"The first fruit of a gifted young pastor, happy [barcode] *old question. It is an excellent choice for sma* *churchwide sermon series."*

—**Janice R. Huie**, Bishop (ret.), Texas Annual Conference,
The United Methodist Church

"Matt Miofsky is one of the brightest and most cutting-edge pastors in the country. His ministry and teachings are insightful, applicable, and practical for everyday living."

—**Emanuel Cleaver III**, Senior Pastor, St. James UMC, Kansas City;
author of *Pastor on Track*

"Matt nails it! He lifts the hood on life and takes apart the engine, showing us what true fulfillment looks like. You need to read this book."

—**Jorge Acevedo**, Lead Pastor, Grace Church, SW Florida;
author of *Vital* and *Sent*

"Matt is one of the dynamic young leaders whose model of ministry I point to at conferences around the country. He is paving the path for effective missional, inclusive, multi-campus ministry in a skeptical post-Christian culture."

—**Mike Slaughter**, Ginghamsburg Church, Tipp City OH;
author of *The Passionate Church*

"Matt Miofsky's voice speaks to new generations who are tired of theology unconnected to their daily lives but who are looking for happiness in all the wrong places."

—**Robert Farr**, Bishop, Missouri Annual Conference,
The United Methodist Church

"Matt possesses great gifts to convey the Word of God in a way that makes people want to integrate it into their daily lives."

—**Rev. Terri Swan**, Senior Pastor, Salem Church UMC, St. Louis, MO

"Matt Miofsky is a pastor and leader who has the ability to cast vision and connect people to Christ. "

—**Olu Brown**, Lead Pastor, Impact Church, Atlanta;
author of *Leadership Directions from Moses*

"Matt Miofsky appeals to the mind and heart by explaining difficult spiritual and emotional concepts in a down-to-earth way. I will be using this book and study as a personal resource and a teaching tool in my congregation."

—**Jacob Armstrong**, Founding Pastor, Providence UMC, Mt. Juliet TN;
author of *Renovate*

happy?
what it is and how to find it

happy?
978-1-5018-3110-2
978-1-5018-3111-9 *eBook*

happy? Leader Guide
978-1-5018-3112-6
978-1-5018-3113-3 *eBook*

happy? DVD
978-1-5018-3114-0

Matt Miofsky

happy?
what it is and
how to find it

Abingdon Press / Nashville

happy?
what it is and how to find it

This book is printed on elemental chlorine-free paper.

Library of Congress Cataloging-in-Publication data has been requested.

ISBN 978-1-5018-3110-2

17 18 19 20 21 22 23 24 25 26 — 10 9 8 7 6 5 4 3 2 1
MANUFACTURED IN THE UNITED STATES OF AMERICA

To my family—Jessica, Caleb, Carly, and George.
You give up much so that I can serve, study,
and write. Thank you.

CONTENTS

INTRODUCTION

INTRODUCTION

Years ago I was in Chicago's Millennium Park, where there was an outdoor art exhibit. The exhibit showed photographs of families from around the world. It spanned continents, income levels, language barriers, and cultural identities, and the images ranged from wealthy families living in grand estates to rural peasants inhabiting thatched-roof hovels. The photographers had asked the parents of each family a question: "What are your hopes for your children?"

The result was surprising. Across all the lines that divide people, across all the contextual and cultural differences, across all the varied backgrounds and lived realities, the answers were shockingly similar: "We want our children to be happy. And we want them to have a better life than we had."

People are different. We have different hopes, dreams, and aspirations. But all of us have one thing in common, something that is close to universal. We all want to be happy.

But what is happiness? Is it the feel-good emotion that comes over us when we are having a good day—when we land that job, get that raise, receive surprising good news, or find a ten-dollar bill in an old coat pocket? Is happiness an emotion that rises and falls depending on how things go on any particular day, week, month, or year? Well, yes; at least that is how many of us think of happiness. But there is a deeper meaning of the word, something that doesn't rise or fall depending on our life circumstances. This deeper kind of happiness is more like a choice, a state of mind, a way of living in the world. It is something we can tap into and experience even on the hardest of days. It goes by many names other than happiness. Some call it joy, others peace. Some call it contentment or inner calm.

In the Old Testament, this kind of happiness is called shalom. Some of you know that Hebrew word well. Most commonly used today as a Jewish greeting, the word is typically translated into English as "peace," but it has a layered and more nuanced meaning. Shalom can be understood as welfare, health, prosperity, well-being, or safety. It is often talked about as wholeness or completeness.

In the New Testament, which was written primarily in Greek, the comparable word is eirene, which also can be translated as "peace." It is the word the angels use in announcing Jesus' birth (Luke 2:14). It is what Jesus leaves with his disciples during the Last Supper, hours before his arrest and eventual death (John 14:27). It is the word Jesus uses to greet his disciples after his resurrection (John 20:19). Paul describes "peace" as the primary mission of Jesus, the essence of the good news (or gospel), and the calling of all Christians (Ephesians 2:14-17, 6:14-15). However the word is translated, it sounds important! God wants us to have it and proclaim it to others.

In addition to the biblical idea of shalom or peace, there is a related word that contributes to my definition of happy. In the Old Testament, the Hebrew word is *echer*. In the New Testament, the Greek word is *makarios*. Both are translated traditionally as "blessed." For those of you new to reading the Bible, there are a dizzying number of translations out there. In the Common English Bible (a translation I will be using primarily in this book and one I recommend to you if you don't have a Bible), these words are often translated as "happy." I'll give you a couple of examples. In the Old Testament Psalms, the entire book starts off with this advice:

> *The truly happy person*
> > *doesn't follow wicked advice,*
> > *doesn't stand on the road of sinners,*
> > *and doesn't sit with the disrespectful.*
> *Instead of doing those things,*
> > *these persons love the LORD's Instruction,*
> > *and they recite God's Instruction day and night!*
> > > *(Psalm 1:1-2)*

In the New Testament, Jesus talks about happiness in a famous series of teachings called the Sermon on the Mount. Here is how he starts:

> *"Happy are people who are hopeless, because*
> *the kingdom of heaven is theirs.*

*"Happy are people who grieve, because they
will be made glad.*

*"Happy are people who are humble, because
they will inherit the earth."*

(Matthew 5:3-5)

In both of these cases, happiness or being blessed is not so much something that people discover or create for themselves but is something given to people by God. Happiness in the Bible is more often a gift to be received than a feeling to find. Happiness is a result of listening to the wisdom of God, paying attention to how we are created and what we are created for, and living in alignment with those purposes.

The problem is that the biblical model for finding happiness is often counterintuitive. It doesn't always come from the places where we look; after all, human beings have a tendency to check the wrong places and employ the wrong means to experience happiness. Many such misguided attempts are recorded in the Bible as well. But, contrary to what some people say, God's desire is not for our lives to be restrictive, boring, or moralistic. God wants to give us a better life than the one we might come up with on our own. God wants us to be happy.

In this book, we are going to explore happiness—not the feeling that comes and goes but the deeper sense of wholeness, completeness, and peace that is described so often in Scripture. It's a contentment that comes not from everything being good in life, but from a God who is present and active at all times and in all circumstances. It is God's desire for you, your family, your friends, our cities, our countries, and indeed our world.

The scriptural meaning of happiness is broad and deep, but for our purposes we will start closer to home. We will explore what happiness is, where it can be found, and how we can keep it in our lives. I hope that what follows is an encouragement to you. As you read it, individually or in a group, my prayer is that it will lead you closer to peace in your own life.

1

NOTHING WILL MAKE

YOU HAPPY

1

NOTHING WILL MAKE YOU HAPPY

All of us want to be happy. But what does that really mean? What is happiness? Where do we find it? How do we keep it?

First, let me clarify something. I'm not talking about temporary feelings. We all have good days and bad days. We're happy sometimes. We're sad sometimes. I'm talking about something deeper and longer-lasting—an abiding peace, satisfaction, purpose, and joy that for many of us seems elusive.

Second, you can find thousands of books, blogs, YouTube videos, lectures, and podcasts about happiness. In fact, when I run into people and mention this topic, almost every one of them says, "Have you read this book?" or "Did you see this study?" We aren't just going to regurgitate popular wisdom on happiness; we will see what the Bible has to say on the subject. And as we saw in the introduction—the Bible says a lot about happiness.

But before we get to scripture, let's start with science and a study on the subject. Dr. Robert Waldinger, a Harvard doctor and researcher, leads the longest and most comprehensive study on happiness ever conducted. Called the Harvard Study of Adult Development, researchers in 1938 began studying and following 238 Harvard undergraduates, measuring a dizzying number of life factors ranging from physical to psychological to financial. Their aim was as simple as it was ambitious: to figure out what actually makes people happy. Waldinger is the fourth leader to follow these men (they later added women) from the time they were young to the time they were old, testing and verifying what made them happy versus what they thought might make them happy. You see, each generation speculates on what will bring happiness, and this generation is no different. We all have life goals. For example, Dr. Waldinger writes:

> There was a recent survey of Millennials asking them what their most important life goals were. And over 80% said that a major life goal for them was to get rich. And another 50% of those same young adults said that another major life goal was to become famous. And we're constantly told to lean into work, to push harder, and achieve more. We're given the impression that these are the things

that we need to go after in order to have a good life.[1]

What's cool is that the study doesn't tell us just what makes for lasting happiness; it tells us what doesn't. So, in the study, how do people's goals work out? Seventy-five years later, have they brought happiness? If they could go back and do it again, would they do anything differently? We will see at the end of the chapter, but before we get there, let me talk about a different study, this one conducted a little further back in time.

A Study Called Ecclesiastes

Believe it or not, nearly three thousand years before the Harvard study, another guy did a similar study. But he didn't study other people; he studied himself. He tried a bunch of different things to see what would make him happy. Then when he was done, he wrote down his findings in a book. The book is called Ecclesiastes, and it is now part of the Hebrew Scriptures, what Christians call the Old Testament.

The rough meaning of Ecclesiastes, originally translated from the Hebrew, is "Teacher." The book is about a man (the Teacher) who decides to conduct a lifelong experiment on happiness and meaning. Now, tradition tells us that the Teacher is King Solomon of the Old Testament. In fact, one legend is that he wrote Song of Solomon as a young man (a book of love poetry), Proverbs as a middle-aged man (a practical and efficient book of wisdom), and he wrote Ecclesiastes as an old man, reflecting on all that he had learned about life. We don't know his identity for certain, but for our purposes let's call him Solomon.

Ecclesiastes is a memoir of sorts. It is the story of Solomon's journey. He set out to learn what life was all about and what made him happy. As with the Harvard experiment, Solomon's approach was to dispel the myths, those things we chase that don't lead to lasting happiness.

Let's survey the Book of Ecclesiastes and, as we might do with any scientific study, we'll look at some of Solomon's hypotheses, findings, and conclusions. After each conclusion, I'll make some comments of my own.

Work

Hypothesis

If I find meaningful work, that will give me lasting happiness.

Findings

> *I hated the things I worked so hard for here under the sun, because I will have to leave them to someone who comes after me. And who knows whether that one will be wise or foolish? Either way, that person will have control over the results of all my hard work and wisdom here under the sun. That too is pointless.... I mean, What do people get for all their hard work and struggles under the sun? All their days are pain, and their work is aggravation; even at night, their hearts don't find rest. This too is pointless.*
>
> *(Ecclesiastes 2:18-19, 22-23)*

Conclusion

Work cannot make you happy because one day it ends, and when it does, no one remembers and no one cares.

Comments

Reading these findings may be tough for some of us. That's because our generation puts a lot of stock in our jobs. I get it. Which one of us doesn't want a job that's fulfilling and joyful? If we're going to spend forty, fifty, sixty hours a week doing something, don't we want our work to make us happy? That stands to reason. And yet Solomon tells us that work, even if it's meaningful, is not the key to lasting happiness. He says it may be a component of happiness, but it's not something that leads to lasting happiness, and he tells us the reason.

Work eventually ends. It is temporary and that means that one day, you will not have it. If you've invested everything you have in your job, if it has been your primary driver of meaning, purpose, and contentment, and then it ends, what happens? Solomon found that when work goes away so will your happiness.

A man in our congregation told me about his experience seeking happiness through work. He was a successful person who had achieved a lot, liked his job, and found a great deal of meaning in it. Then he retired, and all of a sudden he had to figure out a new identity. He told me that one of the most discouraging times was when he went back to the company to visit. He walked down the halls, and there were people who hadn't worked there before, and they had no idea who he was. Many of the projects that he had worked on so hard had been set aside, and people were doing new things. When he got to the place that used to be his office, he saw that all they had done was slide out his name and slide in somebody else's. It all kept going, just without him. It wasn't just that his work had ended, but very quickly people began moving on, new hires didn't remember, and all the stress, anxiety, and long hours seemed forgotten. Maybe you know that feeling.

It's not that work doesn't contribute to our happiness; it does. But even in noble jobs, we grow weary. What Solomon is saying is that work, even meaningful work, doesn't make for *lasting* happiness.

Accumulation

Hypothesis

Accumulating "stuff" can make us happy: money, possessions, achievements, power.

Findings

> *The money lover isn't satisfied with money;*
> *neither is the lover of wealth satisfied with*
> *income. This too is pointless. When good*
> *things flow, so do those who consume them.*
> *But what do owners benefit from such goods,*
> *except to feast their eyes on them? . . . Just as*
> *they came from their mother's womb naked,*
> *naked they'll return, ending up just like*
> *they started. All their hard work produces*
> *nothing—nothing they can take with them.*
> *(Ecclesiastes 5:10-11, 15)*

Conclusion

We can accumulate possessions, but they don't benefit us, and we can't take them with us. As for achievements, we can't accomplish enough to satisfy the longing for something more. And no matter how great we are, there is always someone better.

Comments

Accumulating money, possessions, achievements, power—all these goals involve the same basic problem. We think if we can just get that next thing—whether it's another dollar or another achievement or another rung on the ladder—then that will make us happy. But Solomon says it won't. He tells us, "When good things flow, so do those who consume them." In other words, as soon as you get the thing that you thought you wanted, guess what happens? Your appetite grows and you want something else. And then as soon as you get that next thing, guess what happens? Once again your appetite grows and you want something else. And so the cycle continues.

I call this the hamster wheel effect. You know what I'm talking about, right? I make $30,000 a year now. If I just made $40,000, things would be so much easier. But when I make $40,000, all of a sudden I discover that if I just made $5,000 more, things would be that much better. So on and so forth.

We do that with money all the time. But it's true about other things, too. We do that with houses and apartments. If I just had two bedrooms, or three bedrooms, or fifteen hundred square feet, or two thousand square feet. But every time we get what we think will satisfy us, we discover that our appetite grows and we could use more.

Life isn't about winning
some game. In fact,
there is no game. There
is no winner. There is
no prize at the end.
Accumulation does not
lead to lasting happiness.

It's also true of intangibles. Maybe you're an overachiever. Maybe you're a perfectionist. A lot of us are like that. We tend to see life as a game or a competition, and so we have to be better than other people. Whether it's money or a house or an award, or even just how great our family is, we think that if we can achieve that next thing, somehow we'll be happy.

By the way, this is where the Facebook effect comes in. Researchers have shown pretty convincingly that Facebook fuels our sense of competition with one another, because we tend to post great things—the beautiful picture of our kids, the cool vacation we went on. Every time we see those things on someone else's Facebook page, they make us feel that we need to catch up. If I could have what they have, then maybe I would be happy.

But you know what? It doesn't work. Listen. It really doesn't work.

Solomon discovered what many of us find when we're looking for the accumulation of anything—money, possessions, achievements. If we expect those things to provide us with lasting happiness, we will be disappointed.

Life isn't about winning some game. In fact, there is no game. There is no winner. There is no prize at the end. Accumulation does not lead to lasting happiness.

Pleasure

Hypothesis

I'll seek pleasure. Surely that will make me happy.

Findings:

> *I said to myself, Come, I will make you*
> *experience pleasure; enjoy what is good! But*

this too was pointless! Merriment, I thought,
is madness; pleasure, of no use at all. I tried
cheering myself with wine and by embracing
folly—with wisdom still guiding me—until
I might see what is really worth doing in
the few days that human beings have under
heaven. . . . I refrained from nothing that my
eyes desired.

(Ecclesiastes 2:1-3, 10a)

Conclusion

There aren't enough parties in the world, people to sleep with, or bottles of wine to cover up the longing we feel.

Comments

Seeking pleasure is an easy philosophy to buy into. I've often called this the sex, drugs, and rock 'n' roll approach. It's essentially an escapist strategy, and it doesn't work either.

People say, "I'm just going to do what makes me happy." In other words, whatever feels good and right in the moment, that's what I'm going to do. It sounds so simple—how could we go wrong if we just do what we think will make us happy? But we end up being held hostage to our feelings, so that over the course of a lifetime we're all over the map. Our lives are fragmented, because we've done whatever we thought would make us feel good in that moment on that day. And those feelings are fickle, they change, and often what feels good one night, leaves us feeling the exact opposite the following morning.

I love what Bertrand Russell said about this in *The Conquest of Happines*. Russell was a twentieth-century mathematician, philosopher, and atheist. He wrote about drunkenness being a temporary suicide. This could also be said about having casual sex, getting high, or engaging in any other self-destructive behavior. Those things don't lead to happiness. All they do is give you temporary respite from your unhappiness. It's not lasting.

The Journey to Meaning

The experiments that Solomon described in Ecclesiastes went on. They included novelty, experiences, wisdom, even religion (not faith but religion, many of you who have gone through the motions of church know what I mean). None of these made him happy or gave him meaning. Everything he tried ended in the same place: futility. He began to think the search was hopeless, that life had no meaning at all.

But along the way, something happened to Solomon. The journey began to change him. He decided, most likely late in life, to write down his search and share with others what he had discovered about the meaning of life. His writings are honest, authentic, raw, disturbing, and beautiful. He does not sugarcoat his experiences or offer easy answers. He does not tie everything up neatly at the end or pretend the quest has ended. Instead, he offers us a glimpse into what, with God's guidance, was revealed to him during his search. And ever since that time, people have been wrestling with, arguing about, and finding hope in his story.

For generations the book of Ecclesiastes has been passed down through religious communities and ultimately to us today. It's surprising to see that very little about the search for happiness has changed. Today there are so many of us who want to figure out what life is all about. We're desperately looking for meaning and want to discover something in life that is significant and lasting. We want lives that are more than a blip on the cosmic radar screen. We want to contribute to something bigger than ourselves. We want to make an impact and leave our mark on the world. We want to be happy—truly happy.

In the end, we want our lives to matter and to live with no regrets. As I talk to people, especially young people, I discover a fear that they will come to the end of their journeys with missed opportunities, dead ends, and regrets.

It's a legitimate fear, as Solomon teaches in Ecclesiastes. Too many of us drift through this life, passing on opportunities and procrastinating on possibilities, only to find out that we missed the very thing we had been looking for. The Book of Ecclesiastes wakes us up to the importance of questions about meaning and happiness, and about the journey that such questions provoke. For that reason, I find it to be refreshingly relevant and important for us today.

Solomon's Warnings

In Ecclesiastes, Solomon shared what he had learned about the search for happiness, and he also issued some warnings along the way. In his honest appraisal, he cautioned us that much of what we think about happiness may in fact be flawed. Let's take a look at Solomon's warnings.

Life Is Futile

I often hear stories of people who find they are closest to God when they are out in nature. The majesty of a mountaintop view, the simple beauty of a flower, the refreshing rains that renew springtime plants—all these have led people to deep reflections on the greatness of God.

If you've ever caught moments of the holy through your interaction with God's creation, then it probably comes as no surprise that Solomon begins Ecclesiastes with a reflection on his observation of nature. But it doesn't take long to realize that, for Solomon, nature inspires not a sense of God's greatness, but a sense of life's futility.

> *What do people gain from all the hard work*
> *   that they work so hard at under the sun?*
> *A generation goes, and a generation comes,*
> *   but the earth remains as it always has.*
> *The sun rises, the sun sets;*
> *   it returns panting to the place where it dawns.*
> *The wind blows to the south,*
> *   goes around to the north;*
> *   around and around blows the wind;*
> *   the wind returns to its rounds again.*
> *All streams flow to the sea,*
> *   but the sea is never full;*
> *   to the place where the rivers flow,*
> *   there they continue to flow.*
> *All words are tiring;*
> *   no one is able to speak.*
> *   The eye isn't satisfied with seeing,*
> *   neither is the ear filled up by hearing.*
> *   (Ecclesiastes 1:3-8)*

As his words indicate, Solomon sees in nature a metaphor for life, but it isn't one of grandeur or inspiration. Rather, watching nature makes him tired!

It reminds me of the 1993 movie *Groundhog Day*, starring Bill Murray. The movie's premise is as simple as it is profound. Murray's character, Phil, finds himself waking up each morning to discover that he is reliving February 2. Each day, no one but Phil remembers what had happened during the previous version of the day. At first, Phil sees this as a license to indulge in whatever behavior he wants without ever having to deal with consequences. Why worry about it, since the next morning he will wake up and relive the same day all over again? Soon, though, his initial excitement wears off. The constant repetition of the same day—the same events, the same outcomes—begins to turn Phil toward despondency and despair. What is life's meaning if it doesn't go anywhere, if every day is full of activity without any progress?

It is exactly this realization that dawns on Solomon as he observes the endless and mundane cycles of nature. Each day, the sun crosses the sky, going around and around. Each day, the wind blows from one direction to the other and comes back around again. Each day, rivers flow into oceans and lakes and yet never fill them up. Solomon observes all this activity in nature but never sees it producing anything, never sees it going anywhere. It just repeats itself day after day, season after season, year after year.

Solomon sees in this endless activity a window into a problem that plagues us all. Many of us devote little time to considering where our lives are headed. We take jobs, begin relationships, and start habits without much thought as to where they will take us.

Recently I spoke with a man who for twenty years had worked in a job that he was less than enthused about. It's not that he was unsuccessful; on the contrary, he worked hard and received affirmation from his superiors in the form of promotions and raises. He became prominent in the company and even garnered attention industry-wide. He received awards, his advice was sought out, and he gave presentations to his peers and colleagues. His work rewarded him financially, and he wanted for nothing.

"Why, then," he asked me, "am I not happy?"

We spoke for a while longer, and he admitted that he had never felt these accomplishments were enough. There was always another benchmark to hit, another hill to climb, another competitor to beat. The raises were never quite substantial enough, and the feelings of satisfaction never lasted long enough. His work provided him a lot of activity— in fact, more than he wanted—and yet he had the feeling it wasn't headed anywhere. Like a hamster on a wheel, he was running and running but not getting anyplace.

For many of us, by the time we realize we are running on that wheel, it's too late. We have given away the best years of our lives to something that does not last or lead to where we thought it would. Such is Solomon's warning. Is our activity actually taking us anywhere, or are we on a journey that will take us back to where we started? Has life become futile?

Life Is Familiar

Some people seek happiness in blazing their own trail, believing they can escape the mundane nature of life through novelty, creativity, and innovation.

As a young pastor, I lodged more than my fair share of complaints about the way churches operate. Unnecessary meetings, tired traditions, inward focus—surely God intended more for his church than that. Seeing these flaws and others, I was convinced there had to be a better way, and I discerned a call to start a new church based on creativity, missional focus, and innovatively practicing the ancient faith.

I believe these impulses were from God, but I also know that my pride got in the way. I was proud of being different, of blazing my own way, of "discovering" a way to do church differently. In retrospect, I realize that I was putting my faith less in God's Spirit and more in my own ability.

The church thrived and continues to do so. But if I'm honest, I must admit that certain things about the church I started weren't as innovative as I had hoped. In fact, after just a few short years I found that we were repeating many of the realities I had set out to reform! It seems that the more things change, the more they stay the same.

Such is the nature of Solomon's second warning. Many people stake their hopes on the ability to do something new or different. Solomon himself tried this, only to make a depressing discovery:

> *Whatever has happened—that's what will*
> *   happen again;*
> *whatever has occurred—that's what will*
> *   occur again.*
>
> *There's nothing new under the sun. People*
> *may say about something: "Look at this!*

It's new!" But it was already around for ages before us.

(Ecclesiastes 1:9-10)

Is anything really new? Consider the way that novelty can capture our attention.

In politics, each new group of candidates promises change. And yet, how many politicians before them had made the same claims? Did anything really change? In fashion, what is presented as new and trendy is really just a rehashing of a style many of us (or our parents) remember from twenty years ago. In other fields, young leaders seek to create change, only to realize that similar things have been tried many times before.

Solomon warns us that chasing after new experiences can distract us from dealing with the struggles inherent in life. I have met many people who run far away, move to new cities, quit jobs, and construct countercultural lives, only to discover that they haven't escaped the things they wanted to change. That's because the core questions of life can be camouflaged by novelty but not solved.

As wonderful as new experiences can be, Solomon discovered that, in the end, there is nothing new under the sun. Life is familiar, and no amount of innovation can change that. If we are to make meaning of life and find true happiness, it will need to be through something more than novelty.

Life Is Fleeting

Comedian Woody Allen once quipped, "Life is full of misery, loneliness, and suffering—and it's all over much too soon." Solomon would laugh, because he discovered the same thing. Life, in addition to being futile and familiar, is fleeting. Whatever permanence or meaning we might think we attain, death is the great equalizer. And no legacy, no matter how great, can win us lasting remembrance or importance. Solomon writes:

> *There's no remembrance of things in the past,*
> *nor of things to come in the future. Neither*
> *will there be any remembrance among those*
> *who come along in the future.*
>
> *(Ecclesiastes 1:11)*

Many of us identify meaning with things that last, with a legacy that will live on. In the American presidency, consider the way that emphasis shifts from the first term to the second, from reelection to legacy building. No longer is the primary concern what will I do in the future, but rather how will the future remember what I have already done.

I'm an avid fan of Roman history. It seems that the Roman emperors were concerned not so much with the problems facing the empire as with their own legacy. They erected monuments, memorials, and great edifices. They named cities after themselves. The emperors were widely believed to be the most important people in the world, and yet, despite their power, wealth, ambition, and effort, their names are largely forgotten. Years later, people not only don't remember the emperors' names; most don't care.

Like the emperors, Solomon sought meaning by attempting to establish a reputation that would last. He committed himself to wisdom and tried to live in a sober, measured, and thoughtful way. He avoided wasting his life in folly, believing that living wisely would gain him something lasting. What he discovered, though, was that "this too is pointless. There is no eternal memory of the wise any more than the foolish" (Ecclesiastes 2:15-16).

Today, many of us still believe that meaning can be found in activities or enterprises that will be remembered. As we grow older, it is wise and faithful to turn our gaze toward those who are yet to come. But though it's good to think about one's legacy, it is easy for that impulse to become misguided. When our desire to help shape the future turns into anxiety about being remembered, we are in dangerous water.

In most churches, it doesn't take long to find plaques that memorialize important and faithful people in the community's past. And yet the true legacy of those people, the depth of their faith or their unique desires and dreams, is often lost. What remains is a pew, an altar, a stained glass window. Communities rally around such objects, refusing to change them or, God forbid, tear them down. Is that what most of these faithful people would have wanted? Probably not. But we latch on to physical objects in order to overcome the anxiety that comes with forgetting and being forgotten. What we fail to see is that while the pew may stay, we have drifted far away from the person and the commitments that the pew was meant to memorialize. In an effort to remember, we have placed our hope in an object and a plaque.

This happens all around us. We find plaques in schools, museums, stadiums, and hospital wings. Though many of these memorials will last for decades or even centuries, Solomon's words haunt us. Life is fleeting. No matter how desperately we want to be remembered, it won't bring lasting happiness.

Though it's good to think
about one's legacy,
it is easy for that impulse
to become misguided.
When our desire to help
shape the future turns
into anxiety about being
remembered, we are
in dangerous water.

Solomon's Conclusion

Some of you might be thinking, "All right, Matt, I get it. I get that work doesn't make us happy. Accumulation doesn't make us happy. Pleasure doesn't make us truly happy."

I also get the warnings, and they don't sound like much fun: Life is futile. Life is familiar. Life is fleeting.

But, even after all the hypotheses and warnings, what did Solomon have to say about true happiness? What did he learn from his study?

Here is Solomon's conclusion. He tells us in Ecclesiastes 1:2:

> *Perfectly pointless, says the Teacher, perfectly pointless.*
> *Everything is pointless.*

In other words, as a result of his study, Solomon's grand conclusion is...wait for it...nothing will make us happy.

I know what you must be saying: This is what you're going to leave us with? Nothing makes us happy?

It seems depressing, right? It seems that just like for Solomon, nothing can make us happy either! Now you're likely thinking, "Nothing can make us happy? Matt, I bought this book to find happiness, not to find out it doesn't exist!" Well, don't close the book yet. Stick with me. Because as I was writing Solomon's conclusion over and over again in my notebook, it suddenly hit me: Nothing makes us happy. I tried reading it another way, with a space inserted: No thing makes us happy. No *thing*.

You see, there's a deep truth in Solomon's conclusion. He hints at it later in the Book of Ecclesiastes. After repeating his observation that many things in life are pointless, he goes on to say this:

> *Two are better than one because they have*
> *a good return for their hard work. If either*
> *should fall, one can pick up the other. But how*
> *miserable are those who fall and don't have*
> *a companion to help them up! Also, if two lie*
> *down together, they can stay warm. But how*
> *can anyone stay warm alone? Also, one can*
> *be overpowered, but two together can put up*
> *resistance. A three-ply cord doesn't easily snap.*
> (Ecclesiastes 4:9-12)

While he is going to great lengths to show us that no thing makes us happy, Solomon gives us some hints as to where happiness lies. And it isn't in things, it is in relationships. Solomon tells us that two are better than one, and a three-ply cord doesn't easily snap.

No thing can make us happy, but relationships can.

It's what Jesus taught many years later, and it constitutes one of the simplest and most profound messages of Scripture. Things don't make for lasting happiness; relationships do. The starting point for lasting happiness is relationships, and not just any relationships but three specific kinds of relationships.

Jesus summed it up for us. Somebody asked him what was the meaning of everything in the Old Testament. If you had to boil it all down, what's the point of this whole thing? What would you say it is? And here is what Jesus said. It's recorded in three of the Gospels, though this version happens to be from Matthew.

"You must love the Lord your God with all your heart, with all your being, *and with all your mind. This is the first and greatest commandment. And the second is like it:* You must love your neighbor as you love yourself."

(Matthew 22:37-39)

There are the three relationships. Do you see them?

Do you want to know what makes for lasting happiness, abiding peace, and joy? Jesus taught that it's no thing. It's relationships: with God, with ourselves, and with other people.

Lasting happiness depends on the state of those relationships. It's that simple.

That Other Study

I'm sure some of you are skeptics and aren't buying it. So I want to end today with that other study. Remember it? The Harvard study? I should tell you, I didn't look at it again until I finished writing most of this chapter, including Jesus' great teaching.

Would you like to know what Dr. Waldinger and his colleagues found after seventy-five years of research, after millions of dollars, after thousands of hours of study? Here is what Dr. Waldinger wrote:

> What are the lessons that come from the tens of thousands of pages of information that we've generated on these lives? Well, the lessons aren't about wealth or fame or working

harder and harder. The clearest message that we get from this 75-year study is this: Good relationships keep us happier and healthier. Period.[2]

So, here's your challenge. To the extent that you're investing your time, money, and energy in things, including any of the things we discussed in this chapter, just know that these things may contribute to your happiness, but by themselves they won't enable you to achieve it. Instead, you and all of us should invest every minute of every hour in good relationships with God, with ourselves, and with other people. Those are the things that will bring us lasting happiness. Period.

Gracious God, you know what each of us carries in our lives. You know where we're looking and what we're chasing in our search for happiness. And so, God, today help us listen to the wisdom of so many who have come before us—scientists and philosophers and kings and theologians who say it's not money, it's not work, it's not power, it's not having fun; it's what we invest in good relationships with you, with ourselves, and with other people that brings lasting happiness.

May your Holy Spirit fill us with the wisdom to come back— to listen and learn—and ultimately to live out of the truth that you teach us. We pray these things in the name of the one who came to restore our relationship with you, Jesus Christ our Lord. Amen.

2

THE ART OF FORGIVENESS

2

THE ART OF FORGIVENESS

Lasting happiness comes from good relationships. It sounds so easy, doesn't it? To be happy, invest your time and energy in good relationships. Great.

But it's not quite that simple. The reason is one little word: *good*. True happiness comes not just from relationships, or some relationships, or any relationships. It comes from *good* relationships. But, as we all discover, having good relationships is more easily said than done. Why is that? Why is it so hard to have good relationships?

Think of this. Have you ever dated somebody, or started a new job, or begun a new friendship? Let's take dating. Here's what usually happens. You go on a date with somebody and you like him or her and that's great. And you go out on a second date and a third date. But then all of a sudden that person does something to make you mad. That always happens at some point in a relationship, right? So maybe you talk about it. You get over it. And then it's fine until he or she does it again. And again. And all of a sudden you start to realize that this person has issues.

Have you ever come to that realization? The person has issues, and the issues are messing up your relationship. But think about this: if you're really mature and self-aware, then at some point you realize that—wait a second—I have issues, too! So now there's not just your issues but my issues. And now all of a sudden, *we* have issues.

Issues characterize all our relationships. We have issues, and issues threaten good relationships. And you know what? That's more or less the story of the entire Bible.

The Bible's central story is that God made us. And God made us to be in relationships. But pretty soon we developed issues, and our issues messed up everything. In the Bible, issues are called *sin*. Sin is bad because it wrecks our relationships with God, with ourselves, and with other people. And really, the whole story of the Bible is about God trying to deal with our issues in order to transform our relationships.

If we ever want lasting happiness or a deep sense of joy and peace, then we have to figure out how to achieve good relationships. But good relationships—with God, with ourselves, and with others—all hinge on our ability to accept and practice one simple art.

It's the art of forgiveness. And that's what we'll be exploring in this chapter.

Jesus and Forgiveness

First, let's talk about forgiveness itself. Forgiveness is complicated. It's confusing. People have lots of questions about it.

What does it mean to forgive?

Does someone have to say he's sorry?

Is forgiveness about her or me?

What do I do with anger and the desire for revenge?

Does Jesus really expect me to forgive this person?

I want to forgive, but how do I do it?

What's distinctive about Christian forgiveness?

If we want a definition of forgiveness, we don't have to look further than Jesus, who we might say came for this specific purpose. Jesus preached repentance and forgave sins. This means that his work was not primarily about setting a moral example, loving people cheaply, making people feel okay, or simply being friends. These were not Jesus' primary mission. His mission was all about God's forgiveness that, through him, was available to all people.

By studying the Bible, we can describe several features of God's forgiveness.

Forgiveness can include judgment and anger.

The LORD said to Moses, "I've been watching these people, and I've seen how stubborn they are. Now leave me alone! Let my fury burn

> *and devour them. Then I'll make a great*
> *nation out of you."*
>
> *(Exodus 32:9-10)*

As we watch God's actions with the Israelites, we can see that forgiveness does not necessarily mean denying or minimizing wrongdoing, or ignoring our anger. Even God is described as angry as several points in the Old Testament. A lot of people have trouble with this aspect of God. But think about the corollary in human beings. Is anger bad? I don't think so. In fact, I think it is important that we are able to get angry. Anger is a sign that something is out of whack, that something isn't right. It is OK to be angry. It is what we do (or don't do) with that anger that we need to worry about (and which I will talk about in a minute). God is angry, but as in the passage above, the fury is directed not toward Israel's destruction but toward their refining, and the making of a great nation. But before that can happen, there is an honest admittance about the fact that something went wrong. Similarly with us, forgiveness is more than accepting what happened and moving on; it must include feeling and then working through anger.

Forgiveness is aimed at reconciliation and restoration, but those goals may not be accomplished this side of heaven.

> *God was reconciling the world to himself*
> *through Christ, by not counting people's sins*
> *against them. He has trusted us with this*
> *message of reconciliation.*
>
> *(2 Corinthians 5:19)*

God intends for us to experience reconciliation in relationships. Everything Jesus did was aimed at forgiveness for the purpose of renewed relationship. So the individual act of dealing with anger is not Christian forgiveness unless it has to do with the other person. That is, forgiveness is more than making ourselves feel better or letting go of resentment. It involves actually changing a relationship. It includes an authentic hope that the offender can be converted through repentance and confession. Sometimes we too quickly write off the possibility of reconciliation in a relationship, even one that has been shattered through sin. Reconciliation ought to be an aim and goal of forgiveness. Having said that though, we need to clarify. In my congregation, there are many people who have been victims of abuse, sexual assault, rape, and other deeply traumatic sins. In such cases, reconciliation does not mean returning to a dangerous and harmful relationship. In some cases, the person who has offended us has long since died and, even if we wanted it, reconciliation is not possible. Christlike forgiveness can include the hope for another person's repentance and transformation without actively talking to, seeing, or being in an active relationship with another person. And sometimes, reconciliation is not possible with another person this side of heaven.

Forgiveness is costly.

> *Those who don't pick up their crosses and*
> *follow me aren't worthy of me.*
>
> (*Matthew 10:38*)

To think forgiveness will not cost us something is naive and far too easy. It cost Jesus great suffering and pain. It cost him his pride on many occasions. It cost him sleepless nights in the garden. It cost him his life on the cross. But the cost of forgiveness is worth it, for it can purchase peace, whereas the cost of anger will purchase bitterness.

In our human relationships, forgiveness costs the one doing the forgiving. It costs us mightily in some cases. There is no getting around the fact that when we choose the path of forgiveness, there is hurt that we absorb. Yes, there is a cost to forgiving, but the cost to us and the world for not forgiving is even higher, because through forgiveness comes healing. No matter how difficult forgiveness is, and no matter how illogical it may seem at times, it is a path to our own healing, to the healing of relationships, and ultimately to our happiness. We must seek to forgive in order to be happy.

Obstacles to Forgiveness

It's fine to talk about forgiveness in the abstract. But an issue arises for many of us. We don't actually know how to forgive. We want to forgive. We know we need to forgive. We think we have forgiven, only to find out that the pain and anger of a situation come back again and again to affect us.

In fact, there are obstacles to forgiveness. There are things in our way, things in our hearts that will not allow us to forgive. Let's explore two of those obstacles and talk about how they keep us from forgiving and, as a result, block our happiness. The obstacles are anger and fear.

No matter how difficult forgiveness is, and no matter how illogical it may seem at times, it is a path to our own healing, to the healing of relationships, and ultimately to our happiness.

Anger

At the very beginning of the Bible, in the Book of Genesis, Cain became furious with Abel and it led to murder. In the New Testament, Jesus made the connection between anger and death when he taught his disciples, "You have heard that . . . all who commit murder will be in danger of judgment. But I say to you that everyone who is angry with their brother or sister will be in danger of judgment" (Matthew 5:21-22).

In this passage Jesus is cautioning his listeners about anger, and yet as we saw Jesus himself—and even God—displays anger in other New Testament passages.

> *Then Jesus went into the temple and threw out all those who were selling and buying there. He pushed over the tables used for currency exchange and the chairs of those who sold doves. He said to them, "It's written,* My house will be called a house of prayer. *But you've made it a hideout for crooks."*
>
> *(Matthew 21:12-13)*

> *"Whoever doesn't believe in the Son won't see life, but the angry judgment of God remains on them."*
>
> *(John 3:36)*

All of us, in fact, experience anger. So if anger is important to feel and yet dangerous, then we'd better talk about what to do with it. We can start by reading the Book of Proverbs, in which wisdom is associated with controlling anger on a daily basis.

Fools show their anger at once,
but the prudent ignore an insult.

(12:16 NRSV)

Whoever is slow to anger has great understanding,
but one who has a hasty temper exalts folly.

(14:29 NRSV)

Those with good sense are slow to anger,
and it is their glory to overlook an offense.

(19:11 NRSV)

Proverbs teaches us that when we don't control our anger, we usually dig ourselves into a hole. So, why do we keep doing it? There are lots of reasons. For some people anger is easier than the alternatives of sadness, fear, loneliness, or hard conversations. Often we assume the worst about people. Anger provides us an immediate sense of satisfaction and self-righteousness. There's no shortage of things each day to get angry about, no shortage of justifications, no shortage of people to feed and fuel our anger.

In contrast, God, who does get angry, is described repeatedly in ways such as this:

The LORD is compassionate and merciful,
very patient, and full of faithful love.

(Psalm 103:8)

Anger is our solution to hurt; forgiveness is God's solution. And at some point we must give up our solution and try God's.

Measuring up to God's standard requires a lot of us. In some cases, anger may be necessary and warranted; in other cases, it may not be. We must decide if the situation warrants our anger; maybe it's just not worth it. Every day we suffer little slights, people annoying us, someone cutting us off in traffic, or not following through on something. Not every injustice requires or deserves our anger. In such cases, maybe we can try something different. This may mean moving on, seeing the situation from another's point of view, or in my case, just going to the gym for an hour. Anger is important sometimes; other times, it is just not worth it.

But other times it is right and necessary to get mad. But in those situations, it is important to keep short accounts. This does not mean you shouldn't get angry, just that you should deal with it quickly and decisively. As Paul wrote, "Be angry but do not sin; do not let the sun go down on your anger" (Ephesians 4:26 NRSV). I don't think it literally means that we should never go to sleep angry. Instead, it means that we ought not allow anger to stay in our hearts for too long. When we let small hurts pile up, stay angry without acknowledging it, or push our anger down, it can get lodged there. Paul knew that often we overestimate the cost of dealing with a difficult situation and underestimate the cost of not dealing with it. Not dealing with it causes anger to find a home in our heart. So, while he commends us to get angry, he warns about staying angry, and not working through that anger.

Paul goes on to say, "Put away from you all bitterness and wrath and anger and wrangling and slander, together with all malice, and be kind to one another, tenderhearted, forgiving one another, as God in Christ has forgiven you" (Ephesians 4:31-32 NRSV).

Similarly, James points out that, long term, anger does not help us.

> *Know this, my dear brothers and sisters: every-*
> *one should be quick to listen, slow to speak, and*
> *slow to grow angry. This is because an angry*
> *person doesn't produce God's righteousness.*
> *(James 1:19-20)*

For most of us, getting past the obstacle of anger involves two steps: uncovering your anger, and then putting away anger by deciding to forgive.

Step 1. Uncovering Your Anger

> Each of you must tell the truth to your
> neighbor *because we are parts of each other*
> *in the same body.* Be angry without sinning.
> *(Ephesians 4:25-26)*

"Be angry without sinning"—what an intriguing phrase. Paul feels that some anger is holy and justified, and some isn't. Telling the difference can be difficult, and it is here that we need others. Left to our own, we tend to make two costly mistakes.

First, we are angry about things that are not real offenses. Just because you are mad does not mean another person has actually hurt you. We all know this feeling, of getting angry and then searching for someone to help us justify how we feel. Having someone else in our lives helps us discern the truth of another's behavior.

Second, when our anger is justified, we aren't angry enough. We let people off the hook too easily or make excuses. We try to ignore real hurt or suppress it and blot it out from memory. We think that just forgetting an offense constitutes forgiveness.

So, Paul tells us, be angry, own the anger, understand why you are angry and if it is justified. Then be in it. Paul wants us to feel our anger, without covering it up or justifying it. Can we be present in our anger?

Step 2. Putting Away Anger by Deciding to Forgive

Once we own our anger, how do we deal with it? How many of us parents take it out on our kids or spouse? How many of us use it as a reason to make poor decisions? How many of us self-destruct? How many of us blame ourselves and beat ourselves up? How many of us hold on to anger because, strangely, we have found a certain comfort in it?

Many of us actually want to be angry. That includes me. Anger can mask hurt. It can cover up embarrassment. It can deflect responsibility. It can justify bad behavior. It can push aside feelings of inadequacy, especially for guys. And it begins to kill.

As one therapist and friend of mine said, anger is a self-imposed prison and forgiveness is the only key. When we hold on to our anger we become dependent on it; we don't know how *not* to be mad or victimized. But here is the paradox of anger: other people can cause it, but you are the only one who can solve it. You alone are responsible for your anger.

At some point, however you feel about anger, you have to step back and evaluate its effectiveness. It may seem justified. It may feel good. But is it working for you?

If it isn't, you can choose the path of forgiveness. Notice that it's a path. We can't accomplish it all at once; we must think about it as a course, a road. The bigger our hurt, the more daunting the path is.

The path will include talking with people who have traveled the same road and forgiven others. It will include praying and a fair amount of patience. As we wait, we can do several things. We can accept reality: what happened cannot *un*happen. This is the truth that Paul urged on the Ephesians. But accepting what happened does not mean agreeing to it or condoning it. We can trust in God's approach and not ours. We can turn over control. All of this can lead us toward a willingness to forgive.

Fear

One day, Jesus was talking with the disciples about dealing with sin in community. Peter, looking for rules, asked a question that many of us probably have wondered about.

> *Then Peter said to Jesus, "Lord, how many times should I forgive my brother or sister who sins against me? Should I forgive as many as seven times?"*
>
> *Jesus said, "Not just seven times, but rather as many as seventy-seven times."*
> (Matthew 18:21-22)

Behind the question, we can see that Jesus' teaching on forgiveness made Peter nervous. What do you suppose he was scared of? What are any of us scared of?

Fear of Being Hurt Again

You've heard the old saying: Fool me once, shame on you; fool me twice, shame on me. Many of us won't forgive because we don't want to be hurt again.

Sometimes forgiveness can lead to restoration and reconciliation. In this case, it's true that forgiveness opens us up to being hurt again. Forgiveness comes with this possible cost.

But sometimes forgiveness can lead to a new understanding of the other person, resulting in the relationship being fundamentally changed and given new boundaries. In this case, forgiveness frees us but doesn't necessarily lead to reconciliation.

I think of a young woman I know who went with a friend to confront a family member who had abused her.

> "I told him I was taking back the power I had given him all those years. I told him I loved him and felt sorry for him and hoped if he still had problems he would get help, and that I wasn't looking to have a relationship with him. Then I turned and walked out to the car with my friend. She walked; I floated!"

In this case the woman was not reconciled in the sense that she resumed any kind of relationship with the person. But there was a closure of sorts—a freedom that came from reconciling the situation and forgiving the person. The relationship was changed. It no longer held the same power over her. It was transformed through the power of forgiveness.

Fear of Condoning the Behavior

Some of us fear that if we offer forgiveness, it's as if we're saying this behavior is no big deal—that by forgiving the person, we're saying that what happened was OK.

Here we confuse punishment and forgiveness. We think that if we hold a grudge, somehow we are punishing the other person. But in truth, it only damages us. Forgiveness does not condone behavior or preclude setting new boundaries for our own safety. It does help us to move on.

Fear of Losing Ammunition

Recently at a staff meeting we were talking about forgiveness, and someone said, "If I forgive, I lose my ammunition."

I loved the statement because it was so honest! Think about it. In some situations there is power in being the one hurt, because we can hold it over the one who hurt us. It rings true for me. I can't tell you the number of times that my fights escalate into who has hurt the other one the most.

Then think about what God does. God doesn't hold grudges; rather, God frees us completely. And of course this means that God, unlike most of us, doesn't keep beating us up for the same sin.

The story of the prodigal son is a perfect example. Spotting his sinful son in the distance, the prodigal's father didn't punish him. Instead, the father "saw him and was moved with compassion. His father ran to him, hugged him, and kissed him" (Luke 15:20).

Fear of Losing a Crutch

As time goes by, as grieving happens, as we work through anger, there is a time when part of the identity as victim has to be left behind. But sometimes that's hard because, strange as it may sound, soon we discover there are some benefits to being a victim. People sympathize with us. Friends show us kindness and give us extra attention or even excuses for some of our shortcomings. Here's what one friend told me:

> It's complicated, but for me I allowed this bad thing that happened to me define me. It became a crutch, and it was easy to blame the not-so-great parts of my life on that crutch. Not that being angry and sad and afraid is good, but it's familiar. Sometimes living in darkness is easier, because it's comfortable and familiar.

Accepting God's Forgiveness

Having defined forgiveness and explored obstacles to forgiveness, let's talk about the way forgiveness works in the three kinds of relationships we discussed earlier—with God, with ourselves, and with other people.

In our relationship with God, the guiding Scripture will be one verse. I know that doesn't sound like a lot, but this verse packs a punch. It comes from a letter that Paul wrote to one of the first churches, at a place called Colossae. You may recognize it, because you hear it read at a lot of weddings. The verse is this: "Be tolerant with each other and, if someone has a complaint against anyone, forgive each other. As the Lord forgave you, so also forgive each other" (Colossians 3:13).

That sounds pretty simple, right? But before we get to the meat of that verse, there's one little phrase that we have to grapple with: "*As the Lord forgave you*, so you also forgive each other."

It's so easy to miss that phrase. What it means is that before you can forgive yourself or other people, you first must experience God's forgiveness. There is a connection, in other words, between experiencing forgiveness and the ability to forgive. Our ability to forgive others starts with accepting or experiencing God's forgiveness of us.

And you know what? Really, the whole purpose of Jesus' ministry, if I had to sum it up, was this: to let us know we are forgiven and to change our relationship with God.

In order to understand what Jesus taught, think about what was going on at the time he lived on earth. When Jesus was alive, people of most religions saw God or the gods as powerful beings that had to be appeased, like some sort of cosmic school principal. When you did good things, the principal rewarded you. And when you did bad things, the principal punished you. So, for a lot of people, their relationship with God or the gods was characterized by fear.

Then along came Jesus, and he preached something completely different. In fact, it was so radically different that people had trouble believing him. Jesus said, in effect: You don't have to be afraid, because God knows you have issues. God forgives you and wants you to forgive.

If you can accept Jesus' teaching and experience God's forgiveness, then it totally changes your relationship with God. Paul put it like this in his Letter to the Romans:

> *You didn't receive a spirit of slavery to lead you*
> *back again into fear, but you received a Spirit*
> *that shows you are adopted as his children.*
> *With this Spirit, we cry, "Abba, Father."*
>
> *(Romans 8:15)*

In other words, you don't have to be scared of God. Instead of seeing God as this school principal in the sky, we can think of God as a loving parent who sees us as children.

That's huge. Do you know why? Because, for whatever reason, a lot of us see God's love as being dependent on whether we're doing a good job or a bad job in life. Many of us grew up with the church reinforcing this—when you mess up, God doesn't love you as much, and when you do good, God rewards you.

But Jesus says no. God approaches us with a posture of forgiveness, always and forever. He sees us as children. Look, your friends might not know you have issues. Your family might not know. Coworkers might not know. But God knows. And in spite of those issues, God loves you. You are a child of God—forgiven, valuable, and deserving of happiness.

Forgiving Myself

Experiencing that truth changes not only how we experience God but how we see ourselves. And that's the second part of this progression. Once we've accepted forgiveness in our relationship with God, we can begin offering forgiveness in our own lives.

Recently I preached a whole series on forgiveness. Throughout that series, do you know the question I was asked most frequently? It went something like this: "I'm beginning to understand the concept that God forgives me. But, Matt, how do I forgive myself?"

Some of you ask that same question, right? Interestingly, there's nothing in the Bible that specifically mentions forgiving ourselves. Surely, though, forgiving ourselves is part of what

Jesus meant when, as part of the second great commandment, he taught us to love ourselves: "*You must love your neighbor as you love yourself*" (Matthew 22:39). To be clear, I think that when we say "forgiving ourselves" what we really mean is accepting the forgiveness that God has already given us. It is internalizing, recognizing, and living into the forgivness that is already ours in Christ. That is what I mean when I say "forgiving ourselves."

Paul, in describing sin, touched on a related point worth noting. He wrote, "The wages that sin pays are death" (Romans 6:23).

Do you know what Paul's talking about here? In psychology it's sometimes called "the shame spiral."

We do bad things; we mess up; we sin. Most of us know that. The Bible knows that. God knows that. But instead of realizing that and forgiving ourselves, we feel bad. We beat ourselves up. We experience guilt and shame. That guilt and shame make us feel even worse about ourselves. And when we feel worse about ourselves, we mess up even more. We experience the same shame and guilt, but often intensified because of our repeated self-destructive behavior. This leads us back into shame and guilt, and back into even more self-destructive behavior. We begin to spiral down, all because we haven't accepted what God has freely given to us.

When we're unable to forgive ourselves, it plays out in all sorts of ways.

For some of us, it turns into a need to be needed. We all know somebody like that in our lives. Maybe that person is us. We constantly, constantly pour ourselves out for others, trying to be martyrs in the desperate hope that they will love us, because we don't love ourselves.

For some of us, it turns into perfectionism: if I can just do everything right, always and every time, maybe I can prove that I'm good enough, and then people will love me.

For some of us it turns into self-destructive behavior. We beat ourselves up and then do stupid things. So we beat ourselves up some more and do even more stupid things.

For some of us, it's self-sabotage. We sabotage good things in our lives because we don't feel we deserve them.

Whatever our particular version is, when we can't forgive ourselves it keeps us from moving forward.

And yet, do you know what the Bible says? In 2 Corinthians 5:17, Paul tells us, "If anyone is in Christ, that person is part of the new creation. The old things have gone away, and look, new things have arrived!"

In Christ, each of us becomes a new person. We can see ourselves differently. We don't have to be held back by our mistakes, our screwups, our sins, our shortcomings. God has forgiven us, so we can forgive ourselves. We don't have to beat ourselves up anymore. Christ already died for our sins, so we don't have to keep punishing ourselves.

I share this because I know that some of you have such a difficult time with this. Some of you are so hard on yourselves, beating yourselves up over things that God has long since forgiven.

Now, keep in mind that God's forgiveness doesn't mean we're off the hook. It doesn't mean we stop trying to change. But it does mean we stop punishing ourselves, stop being defined by our mistakes, stop trying to prove ourselves, stop being prisoners of our past.

All of us need to accept God's forgiveness for ourselves, because when we experience God's forgiveness, we can forgive ourselves. And that, in turn, opens the way for the third step in the progression: forgiving other people.

Forgiving Others

Some people struggle to forgive themselves. And surprisingly, in talking to people, I've learned that a lot of them don't feel a pressing need to forgive others. They might say, "I don't have people I'm mad at. I don't have people I need to forgive." But I want to push back on that. All of us could stand to practice forgiveness each and every day.

Let's reread that Colossians passage, and you'll see what I'm talking about: "Be tolerant with each other and, if someone has a complaint against anyone, forgive each other. As the Lord forgave you, so also forgive each other."

Be tolerant with each other. That's a whole different level of forgiveness, a level we may not even think of as forgiveness. Paul is saying, "Look, just learn to put up with each other. Lay off each other a little bit. Give each other more grace and love. After all, you have issues and God deals with those. So maybe you can cut some slack with other people's issues."

By the way, this passage speaks to me all the time. Just about every day when I take my kids to school, one of them forgets something that's critically important, like that day's lunch or some homework. And it's so easy for me to get mad at my child. Well, about a week ago we were all set to go to school, and I realized I didn't know where my keys were. This was bad not only because I had no way to get my kids to school, but because now my kids got to make fun of me for losing something. I had to scramble, call a neighbor. We had to work it all out. My keys were missing for a week. Well, when I finally found them, a funny thing happened. I was able to show more grace toward my kids. When they messed up, I was able to lay off them just a little bit.

Has this ever happened to you? When we're confronted with our own issues, we find it easier to show grace to somebody else.

What Paul is saying in Colossians is that when we come to an understanding of our own need for forgiveness and the own truth of our forgiveness, it transforms how we're able to approach other people. And it does that in all sorts of ways. For example, it transforms small interactions that we have each and every day. All of sudden we can just deal with more. Our tolerance is higher.

OK, think of this. Maybe you're not super mad at anybody, but you walk around with a low level of annoyance all the time. Drivers annoy you. Slow checkers at the store annoy you. The coworker who won't stop talking annoys you. It's so easy to go around with a low level of annoyance. But when we adopt a forgiving lifestyle, we begin to approach other people with a little more grace. Instead of a critical, negative posture toward others, we begin to see that maybe they're not so different from us.

Of course, it's fine to talk about tolerance, about putting up with annoyances and minor hurts in our relationships. But some of you reading this have had big things happen to you. I mean, big, awful, terrible things. How do we work through those? It takes a deeper level of forgiveness.

When we suffer terrible hurts, the natural inclination is to let anger lodge in our hearts and become resentment or bitterness. But over time we realize that the only person hurt by that anger is us. Forgiveness—or even a willingness to forgive, an attempt to forgive—allows us, through God's grace and some hard work, to let go gradually of that bitterness or resentment. It means that we don't have to hang on to anger anymore. We can feel it, but we can release it. Maybe that doesn't fix the relationship, but it allows us to move forward in other relationships with freedom and joy. It moves us one step further along the road to happiness.

Changing Our Relationships

Once we cultivate a willingness to forgive ourselves and others, we turn over to God the need for revenge, the need to control the behavior or emotions of the other person, the need to speed up our healing. Once we give those things to God, we are free to do something different with our anger, to gain a new perspective.

Remember, what we're talking about here is seeking happiness through good relationships, and good relationships through forgiveness. By trying to forgive people who harmed us, we have a chance to change our relationships with them. Keep in mind, however, that we're not in control of the process, and in fact the process can lead to several outcomes:

- Sometimes forgiveness leads to reconciliation and restoration of a relationship to what it ought to be or should have been. (This is certainly true in marriages that heal.)

When we suffer terrible
hurts, the natural
inclination is to let
anger lodge in our hearts
and become resentment
or bitterness. But over
time we realize that the
only person hurt by
that anger is us.

- Sometimes forgiveness means being able to stop hating the other person, to hope for his or her reconciliation to God and authentic transformation and to change the way we view the person even if we maintain a healthy separation from him or her.
- And sometimes forgiveness does nothing more than give us the ability to be in the same room as the other person without going nuts.

Our willingness to forgive sets in motion a process that's beyond our control. But there are some things we can control, and these can help us and perhaps even the person we want to forgive.

Change Our Perspective on the Offender

If you pay attention to Jesus' ministry, he was constantly asking people to see others through a different lens, from a different perspective. Take, for instance, the story of the adulteress in John 8:1-11. The woman clearly was guilty. Adultery was a sin. It went against the word of God. It hurt people. It destroyed families. But as the crowd gathered to stone her, Jesus said, "Whoever hasn't sinned should throw the first stone" (8:7).

He didn't tell the people they couldn't do it or it was wrong; he simply offered them a different perspective. Instead of seeing the woman's sin, they saw their own. Their anger dissipated. One by one the protestors slipped away.

Cultivate Compassion

The idea of feeling compassion for someone who has hurt you may sound crazy. But Jesus, in one of his more controversial teachings, taught that very thing.

> *You have heard that it was said,* You must
> love your neighbor *and hate your enemy.*
> *But I say to you, love your enemies and pray*
> *for those who harass you so that you will be*
> *acting as children of your Father who is in*
> *heaven. He makes the sun rise on both the*
> *evil and the good and sends rain on both the*
> *righteous and the unrighteous. If you love only*
> *those who love you, what reward do you have?*
> *Don't even the tax collectors do the same? And*
> *if you greet only your brothers and sisters,*
> *what more are you doing? Don't even the*
> *Gentiles do the same?*
>
> (Matthew 5:43-47)

Love your enemies? Why would Jesus suggest such a thing? Love is such a strong word. He could have said, "Don't hate your enemies," or "Try not to feel anything toward them," or "Stop thinking about them," or "You don't have to like them." But he didn't. Instead he said to love them.

I think there is practical wisdom in Jesus' words. I have asked people how they feel toward someone who has hurt them, and sometimes they will say, "I don't feel anything."

If we gain perspective on people who have wronged us, then we may begin to feel compassion for them. Compassion means "to suffer with them." It doesn't mean we excuse them or even lighten our judgment; rather, we lament for them and begin to hope for them. Sometimes compassion is authentic concern, a desire that they get help, and sometimes it's just understanding where the other person is coming from.

Dwelling on, praying for, and working on compassion toward our enemies—as difficult as that task may be—slowly begins to shift the feelings we have toward the other person. We begin to move from hatred to something else, something new, and something that can make reconciliation or tolerance or even happiness possible again.

Give a Gift

Giving a gift sounds like the most bizarre thing we could do. Why would we give a gift to someone who has hurt us?

> *"You have heard that it was said,* An eye for an eye and a tooth for a tooth. *But I say to you that you must not oppose those who want to hurt you. If people slap you on your right cheek, you must turn the left cheek to them as well. When they wish to haul you to court and take your shirt, let them have your coat too. When they force you to go one mile, go with them two. Give to those who ask, and don't refuse those who wish to borrow from you."*
>
> (Matthew 5:38-42)

Why do you suppose Jesus would suggest these counterintuitive responses? The last thing most of us would ever want to do for people who hurt us is give them something else. But consider this. One of the worst outcomes of being sinned against is the loss of power. When something is taken from us, it makes us feel out of control, powerless, and at the mercy of another. But when we *give* another person something, especially after she or he takes something, it can reverse the situation. It breaks the power cycle, putting the victim in a role of power. It also stops the cycle of anger and revenge.

Through work with incest victims, one social scientist discovered that the most powerfully transformative act of forgiveness includes a real gift. In some cases it is a physical object; in many cases it is an emotional gift, such as a prayer or flowers on a grave; in other cases it may simply be the words *I forgive you.*

If we are able to change our perspective, cultivate compassion, or give a gift, then often something powerful happens: we can begin to accept our pain and even find meaning in it. As Christians, our tradition maintains this tension: we don't seek pain, and certainly we don't will it on others, but when we experience pain and are able to accept it as our reality, we can find incredible meaning in it.

In his book *Man's Search for Meaning,* Austrian psychiatrist and Holocaust survivor Viktor Frankl argues that meaning can be found in suffering, even extreme suffering. What this says to me is that God can redeem our pain; God can buy it back and use it constructively in our lives. God doesn't cause this suffering. God doesn't will this suffering or desire it for us. But God is powerful enough not to allow our suffering to define and defeat us. God can restore us and can turn our lowest point into our defining moment. In such cases our pain can be an offering to others and to the world. It can connect us with those who have been hurt; it can give our life purpose; it can lead to a sense of purpose, and in the overcoming of pain, we can experience deep and abiding fulfillment and joy.

Amazingly, miraculously, when we face our pain and hurt, when we face the brokenness in our lives and in our relationships, doing so causes us to heal and, ultimately, can bring us happiness.

Maybe It's Time

So, here's where we end up. The reason most of us go through life unhappy is because of messed-up relationships. And the reason a lot of us struggle with messed-up relationships is that it's hard for us to deal with brokenness. But God, in Jesus, gives us this beautiful gift of forgiveness and then asks us to reflect it in every encounter of every relationship in every area of our lives. When we're able to make peace with God, experience forgiveness, and accept that forgiveness, then it changes the way we view other people. And so forgiveness and a forgiving lifestyle become key ingredients in finding lasting happiness.

As we close this chapter, think about those three relationships—with God, with ourselves, and with other people. Maybe there's one that you need to work on.

Maybe some of you need to experience God's forgiveness and realize that God loves you in spite of your issues. Maybe some of you—a lot of you, I suspect—need to forgive yourselves, to just let go, stop beating yourselves up, and start seeing yourselves as God sees you. Today can be the start of a new creation, a new person. And then maybe, finally, it's time to let go of a disagreement we've had with someone. Maybe it's time to show that person a little grace and love, because we realize that person has issues just like we have. Maybe the grace and love you offer aren't little at all, but huge. Maybe they can transform your marriage or your friendships or the way you see your coworkers. Maybe you can stop being mad all the time, because you know what? It's really hard to be happy if you're always mad.

Maybe there's some area of your life today where God is calling you to a lifestyle of forgiveness, because when we're able to forgive, it changes our relationships. It makes those broken relationships good again. And good relationships can lead to lasting happiness.

Gracious and holy God, we struggle to accept your forgiveness, to forgive ourselves, and then to forgive others. We pray that today, healing can take place in some small way. Maybe it starts with a prayer. Maybe we ask for help. Maybe we speak a word and make amends with another person.

Whatever it is, God, we pray that your spirit would prompt us not only to hear this challenge but to practice it in our lives. God, help us to accept your forgiveness and to mirror that forgiveness in our encounters with others. We pray these things in the name of the one who came to forgive, Jesus Christ our Lord. Amen.

3

BEYOND CIRCUMSTANCES

3

BEYOND CIRCUMSTANCES

Lasting happiness comes from good relationships with God, with ourselves, and with other people. As we've seen, an important step on the path to good relationships is learning to forgive. But there's a pitfall along the way: the illusion that happiness is related to circumstances. To put it another way, lasting happiness involves the ability to cultivate contentment in our lives, regardless of circumstances. This is a key difference between the typical way in which our world uses the term "happy" and the biblical idea of lasting happiness. Remember, we're not talking about the emotion of happiness, about the kind of feeling that comes and goes. We're talking about something deeper.

Scripture uses a variety of words to describe this kind of happiness: an abiding sense of peace, hope, joy. And the promise of Scripture is that we can find this deep level of contentment independent of circumstances—whether we're having a good day or an awful day, whether things are great or we're in one of our life's darkest seasons.

Paul's Dark Season

Paul wrote about this challenge during a particularly hard period in his own life. Paul, a preacher and teacher, was one of Jesus' greatest apostles. He started dozens of churches and wrote letters to a number of them. One letter was to the church at Philippi, a city in Asia Minor. In many ways, the church there was the crown jewel of Paul's churches.

The circumstances of the letter are important to understand. Paul was in prison, most likely in Rome, facing capital punishment if found guilty. He did not yet know what the outcome would be, and many of his churches and the people who loved him were understandably worried. I love this letter, because it's really about seeing difficult circumstances from a new perspective. He writes to those worried about him:

> *Be glad in the Lord always! Again I say,*
> *be glad! Let your gentleness show in your*
> *treatment of all people. The Lord is near. Don't*
> *be anxious about anything; rather, bring up*
> *all of your requests to God in your prayers and*
> *petitions, along with giving thanks. Then the*

peace of God that exceeds all understanding will keep your hearts and minds safe in Christ Jesus....

I'm not saying this because I need anything, for I have learned how to be content in any circumstance. I know the experience of being in need and of having more than enough; I have learned the secret to being content in any and every circumstance, whether full or hungry or whether having plenty or being poor. I can endure all these things through the power of the one who gives me strength.

(Philippians 4:4-7, 11-13)

This is one of Paul's most hope-filled, joyous letters. In fact, it's often called the Letter of Joy. And yet it was written during one of the most difficult periods of his life. Paul, sitting in prison, doesn't know what his future holds, but things are not looking good. He's being punished for the very thing he felt God was calling him to do. He has given up everything to listen to God's call on his life. He has several reasons why he could be bitter, resentful, and angry. Instead, in the midst of this incredibly dark season, Paul writes, "Be glad in the Lord always!" He urges the Philippians to seek the peace that surpasses all understanding (biblical happiness).

Instead of seeing imprisonment as an impediment to his ministry, Paul views it as a way of helping to spread the gospel. He lists good things that have come from the imprisonment:

- The imperial guard is converted.
- Because the guards are people of consequence, word will spread.
- Being faithful when things aren't going your way is inspiring to others.
- Other people are now defying authority and being bolder in their faith.

Note that Paul does not say that being in prison is good. He doesn't want to be in prison or even believe that prison is necessarily God's will. He is not denying the difficulty of the situation. But he is claiming that through the power of God the imprisonment can result in good things. This difference is crucial. God does not cause bad things to happen to us; rather, God is present and creating good even in our bad circumstances—if we have the eyes to see it.

Some of the most inspiring moments in my ministry have occurred when I've seen people offer hope to others, not out of abundance but out of pain. Each Easter all of the sites of our church come together for one worship service, and we celebrate the resurrection of Jesus together. Nearly each year, we include as part of that service a powerful testimony of someone who has experienced the redeeming and renewing power of Jesus. Several years ago, I asked my good friends, Mark and Jenn, to share their story. The prior year, they lost their son Ollie to a congenital heart defect discovered shortly after his birth. For nearly all of Ollie's thirteen months, he was in and out of hospitals and doctors' offices. After much prayer, and several moments of hope, Ollie died shortly after Christmas. It was not the way they expected their story to end.

Mark and Jenn had every reason to be crushed in spirit (and they were). They had every reason to be angry at God, to give up on faith, and to blame God for what had happened to their son. Instead, they decided to choose hope. After much prayer and many conversations with me and others, they came to believe that God didn't cause Ollie's death—but he could bring about good from it. They knew that they had a choice— they could choose bitterness and anger, or they could choose joy and hope. They chose the latter.

Mark and Jenn decided to begin a nonprofit benefiting congenital heart defect research and serving other families who had children born with this defect. To date, their nonprofit has raised hundreds of thousands of dollars and impacted the lives of hundreds of families. Jenn uses her story to provide counsel, comfort, and hope to other parents. That Easter service, Mark and Jenn sat before thousands of people and shared their journey from the darkest hour of their life to a place of joy and hope. They still mourn Ollie's death daily. They would do anything in their power to change that outcome. They also have experienced the abiding presence of God who has used their darkest hour to provide hope and comfort to many others. By participating in this work, Mark and Jenn can have confidence that Ollie's life not only mattered, but is still impacting many. Would they change this if they could? Absolutely. But in the midst of great tragedy, Mark and Jenn have found through their faith a peace that surpasses understanding, a joy that is not dependent on their circumstances but on the promises and power of God.

Patience, endurance, resolve, conflict resolution, resourcefulness, creativity—all these can result from trying situations.

Think of Paul. How is it that he was able to maintain joy and an abiding sense of peace even when he was in prison? What was his secret? What did he figure out? And how can we make use of it in our own lives, no matter the circumstances?

Let's talk about four keys to lasting happiness in your life as it is, not as you wish it to be. The keys are to live in the present, change your perspective, be grateful, and let go.

Live in the Present

Paul gives the Philippians some simple but powerful advice: "Don't be anxious about anything" (4:6).

Two of the greatest obstacles to lasting happiness are regrets about the past and anxiety about the future, because they make it difficult to see what the present is already offering us.

Eastern religious traditions talk a lot about this idea. One quotation that is sometimes attributed to the Buddha says, "Do not dwell on the past. Do not dream of the future. Concentrate the mind on the present moment." Maybe you've heard this practice described as mindfulness, learning to live in the moment, embracing the now, or learning to be in the present.

It's interesting that Jesus said much the same thing when he told his disciples, "Stop worrying about tomorrow, because tomorrow will worry about itself. Each day has enough trouble of its own" (Matthew 6:34).

Being in the present moment reduces anxiety, points us to missed opportunities, wakes us up to what is already true about our lives, and helps us maintain joy even in less-than-ideal situations.

Two of the greatest
obstacles to lasting
happiness are regrets
about the past and
anxiety about the future,
because they make it
difficult to see what the
present is already
offering us.

Let me use a mundane example. I am impatient. I hate waiting, and even more than that I hate waiting when I don't expect to wait—long lines, flight delays, traffic jams, or, the absolute worst, waiting in the line at the grocery store while someone writes a check (I am only half kidding here). When I am forced to wait when I didn't expect it, I immediately start obsessing about where I need to be. I think of what else I could be doing or need to be doing. But instead of getting mad, I've tried to use those moments to be mindful. I use them to pray. I have a devotional app on my phone. I've started using these moments as signs from God that perhaps I need to stop, read a Scripture, say a small prayer, or simply pay attention to what God may be trying to show me in the situation. I learn to be present instead of focusing on where I'm not. It's a small step, but it feels meaningful and it transforms a less-than-ideal situation into moments ripe with opportunities to hear from God. It's simple but substantive. It turns my frustrating moments into more joyful ones.

Most of us view our lives chronologically, with the future as a mystery. We don't know what lies over the next hill, and therefore we are frightened and anxious. Scripture encourages us by sharing the beginning of our story, as well as its glorious end: Jesus was crucified, rose from the dead, and will come again. God promises that same future to us. What this means is that we can have confidence that whatever happens next, we are people who know the end of the story. We know the victory that ultimately awaits us. We know that whether things go well or not in a certain season of our lives, God has our future secure. And we can experience joy and peace now, not based on the season of life we are in, but rooted in the future that we know is secure in God.

Paul, while in prison, is able to view the future differently because of his faith. He wants to survive his imprisonment. He thinks this will happen and undoubtedly prays for it. But he also knows that, while death and tragedy may win the battle, they have already lost the war. Paul says this grand truth is what fuels our ability to see things differently. And seeing things differently is a step on the path to lasting happiness.

Change Your Perspective

In Paul's Letter to the Philippians he writes, "I have learned the secret to being content in any and every circumstance, whether full or hungry or whether having plenty or being poor" (4:12).

What Paul means, I believe, is that he has experienced a range of circumstances and remembers that his life has been both better and worse than it is now. That range has changed his perspective. Such a change is something all of us can use, because our perspective can become warped.

Sometimes I get locked into seeing a problem, a challenge, or a difficulty from just one viewpoint. When that happens, I usually try to buckle down, grind it out, and push through the problem. But often what I really need is to step back, stop trying so hard, and get a new perspective.

Remember those pictures that can be seen two ways? You know, one way it's a young woman, and another way it's an old woman; one way it's a candlestick, and another way it's two people facing each other. From one perspective, it might be a staircase going down, from another it may look like one that is going up. When we get a new perspective, sometimes we can see the same circumstance in an entirely new way. Everyone from artists to photographers to inventors to leaders has experienced this.

One thing I love about Paul is that he is incredibly human. There's no shortage of passages showing Paul complaining about, criticizing, and name-calling his enemies. But as he sits in prison, a changed perspective allows him to see his jailers differently, and he ends up converting them to Christ. Paul did the same thing throughout his ministry. He was able to look past the bad things people said about him and his clear dislike of some of them to see what they had in common: Christ.

I fear we have not yet learned Paul's lessons. We have friends who disappoint us, coworkers who get under our skin, competitors who badmouth us. It's easy to get brought down by people we don't like.

As a pastor, I've learned that I have my fair share of critics. And guess what? There are pastors I don't like either, who have said unkind things about me, or with whom I've strongly disagreed on a range of issues. Early in my ministry, another pastor criticized me personally. I was angry, because the comments seemed unfair. I wanted so badly to set the record straight. But then a friend advised me, "If you try to chase down and correct everything that people say about you, there won't be enough time for the work you want to accomplish and that God has called you to do. Besides, there's usually a kernel of truth in every criticism." That comment changed my perspective. Today I try to see critics in a different, even helpful way. I may not like what they have to say. Heck, I may not like them! But I also try to remember that I cannot correct every misunderstanding, and maybe in their criticism there is some truth. Instead of being defensive, I can use even these potentially deflating moments as opportunities to grow.

There is another set of practices prevalent in our culture that tends to warp our perspective: comparison and competition. We tend to envy those we think have more or better than we have, whether it's money, house, family, or well-behaved kids. Maybe we envy someone for whom things seem to have worked out, or for whom things seem to be going great—the friend who becomes engaged while we're still looking for someone, the family that appears to be happy when ours feels strained, the person whose career path seems smooth while ours is bumpy. I could go on and on, and sometimes I do.

When we make this kind of comparison and competition a habit, our perspective can become warped. We begin to think that somehow our lives don't measure up or aren't where they should be. When this happens, we need a perspective shift.

For some, the perspective shift involves remembering where we came from. For some, the shift means simply looking around, escaping our tunnel vision, and realizing that things may not be as bad as we had thought.

Recently I traveled to Mozambique, where our church partners with The United Methodist Church in that country to dig wells for clean water. Over the years, I have gotten to know leaders of churches in villages that are scattered across that country. When someone from the US travels there, one cannot help but see life in a new way. The disparity in resources is a wake-up call to me that our world has lots of people in a wide range of circumstances, and in fact that the majority of people on this earth have far less than I do. We tend to lose sight of this if we're constantly comparing ourselves with people who we think have more.

Looking outside our immediate circle of friends, and paying attention to people all over our city, state, and even world can help us shift perspective. If we look closely, we'll find, ironically, that many people are in far more difficult circumstances and yet are happier than we are.

What all of this has in common is this: We can see the same set of circumstances in different ways. We can see the ways in which they bring us down or leave us disappointed. We can also see the possibility and potential in them, and how God can use them to move us forward.

Cultivating contentment means not giving in to the circumstances in your life. It means not accepting suffering or hardship as God's will. It means not losing the drive to see your situation improve. It means not letting your circumstances sap your joy or allowing negative circumstances or people to bring you down. And an important step on that road is gaining a new perspective, learning to see the same set of circumstances differently.

Be Grateful

Sometimes we fall into the trap of thinking, "I would be happy...

> ...if I had a new job."
> ...if I had more money."
> ...if I had a boyfriend or girlfriend."
> ...if my health were better."
> ...if things would only go my way."

We live in an if/then culture. We think our happiness is dependent on our circumstances, and we chase those circumstances from one end of our lives to the other. Sadly, we never seem to catch up with them.

Paul's solution can be found in the passage we read earlier:

> *Be glad in the Lord always! Again I say, be*
> *glad!…Don't be anxious about anything;*
> *rather, bring up all of your requests to God in*
> *your prayers and petitions, along with giving*
> *thanks. Then the peace of God that exceeds*
> *all understanding will keep your hearts and*
> *minds safe in Christ Jesus.*
> *(Philippians 4:4, 6-7)*

Do you see it? Paul's solution is to be grateful, not sometimes, but always! Gratitude is the antidote to if/then thinking. Instead of focusing on what we don't have, we should focus on what we do have. The solution is simple but powerful.

In preparation for a message once, I threw out a question on Facebook: how do you maintain joy when you're having a bad day, week, or year? The most frequently cited answers involved gratitude: Matt, I keep a gratitude journal. Matt, I count my blessings. Matt, every day I find one thing to thank God for. Matt, I remember all the people God has placed in my life.

Gratitude, whatever form it takes, is connected to lasting happiness. Even a cursory Google search will find countless studies from social science to psychology citing gratitude as a practice linked to happiness. Being grateful dramatically increases our chances of happiness, even when things aren't going our way.

Gratitude helps us remain focused on the present and mindful of what we have. It isn't about ignoring the pain in our lives; it's about recognizing our blessings. It allows us to see the ways God is working and walking with us, not the ways God is absent or failing us.

Gratitude works in the midst of small, everyday situations. Have you ever talked with a friend who pointed out all the things that were going badly? Then have you talked with another friend who pointed all the things that were going well? Which friend did you feel better talking to? Who do you want to hang out with? Gratitude is contagious and impacts the people around you. On the flip side, negativity is like a black hole that can suck away our joy. I have never heard anyone regret being grateful.

Gratitude also works in some of the darkest periods of our lives. This past year I conducted a funeral service for a friend, Laura Wiley. Laura, her husband, Tom, and their two young children all come to our church. Laura died at age forty-two after a courageous battle with cancer. Laura was remarkable in countless ways, but she absolutely transformed the lives of hundreds of people simply by the way she dealt with her declining health, and eventually her death. Cancer may have taken her body, but it never, ever stole her joy. She never let it define her perspective. She daily would actively choose joy over anger, and hope over despair. She was relentless about not allowing cancer to take what it had no ability to take: her peace, joy, and happiness. And you know what? She did it. She beat cancer. Cancer never took those parts of Laura.

Among the many people she inspired was her own husband, Tom. Laura imparted to him a perspective of joy in the midst of hardship. I spoke with Tom shortly after she died. I was expecting him to be angry, to express resentment

Gratitude is contagious
and impacts the people
around you. On the flip
side, negativity is like a
black hole that can
suck away our joy.
I have never heard anyone
regret being grateful.

or even disappointment in God (by the way, all of those emotions are fair, and at times, I suspect Tom felt them). But instead, here is what he told me: "I am grateful I have such a strong community of people around me. Most folks don't have neighbors and friends like these." Hours after losing his wife, he was naming that which he was grateful for. It is an incredible sign of faith (and a wife who modeled the same perspective so bravely). Even in his darkest moments, Tom was saying what he was grateful for, almost as if that impulse were second nature. To this day, Tom has actively maintained a perspective of gratitude and chosen joy.

How often do you say what you're grateful for? How often do you find some time when things are great, or even when things are tough, to stop and see what is instead of what isn't? Maybe you should try that before going to bed each night. Write down a few things that happened that day for which you're grateful. After a while, gratitude may become a habit.

Let Go

Part of what makes us unhappy is that we lack the ability to control things, and yet we continue to think we can. We map out our future, time lines and all. We come up with our preferred outcomes. We know when things should happen and how life should unfold. Then we are disappointed when life doesn't play out as we had hoped (by the way, we do this in relationships as well).

We can't control the actions of others. We can't control the economy. We can't control our kids, though we certainly try. We can't control death or disease. Many things are simply beyond our control, so we must learn to accept what we can and can't do. We have to place trust in something or someone beyond us.

I live in the Midwest, where we are blessed with four distinct seasons, plus the transitions between seasons. A cold winter breaks into spring, and it begins to rain... a lot. You know that the cool, wet spring is ending when you wake up to summer's sticky humidity. The first day you put on a jacket to fend off the chilly breeze, you know that fall has arrived. Morning frost is a sure sign that winter is coming. Growing up here, I have come to appreciate each season. They are different; each offers positives and negatives. There are certain activities that you can only do in certain seasons. Each season offers something different. And you know what? I've learned that I cannot control the seasons, but what I can do is learn how to live in each season. This I can control.

Invariably I will meet people who bemoan the seasons. Some spend all winter complaining about the overcast skies. Others gripe about the summer heat and long for the cool, crisp fall weather. Some hate the muddy springs. There are people who want every day to be cool and breezy or warm and sunny. But the seasons don't work that way, and no amount of complaining or bemoaning or praying will change them. We cannot control the seasons; we can only live in them as well as we can.

In the Book of Ecclesiastes, Solomon teaches that just as nature has seasons, so does a human life. He famously writes, "There's a season for everything and a time for every matter under the heavens" (3:1). He goes on to name the seasons—a time for birth, a time for death, a time for planting, a time for harvesting, a time for tearing down and one for building up, and so on. I love this idea of life seasons. I know we'd like to believe we're in control of our life seasons and that we are always progressing onward and upward toward our goals. But we don't have this kind of control, and these unrealistic desires cause many of life's frustrations.

As an alumnus and member of my undergraduate college's admissions process, I have the chance to interview prospective students. Each time I meet one of these extraordinarily bright eighteen-year-olds, I am struck by how much they have thought about the future and how confident they seem to be about it. They will go to college, major in biology, attend medical school, graduate at the top of their class, and land a top residency (on one of the coasts, of course). Then, after establishing themselves for a couple of years, each of them will meet and marry a bright, wonderful, talented person. The two of them will travel and enjoy each other for a few years, and then kids will enter the picture. You get the idea.

Hyperbole aside, all of us plot out our futures at various times in our lives. But we can't predict our life seasons, any more than we can control nature's seasons. What happens when a person loses a job and finds that the career she had prepared for is no longer a possibility? What happens when the person one imagines spending the rest of his life with leaves unexpectedly? What happens when, a year before retirement, the stock market tanks and takes one's 401(k) with it? What happens when someone a person loves dies?

Much of the time, our response is to lament the unfair nature of life or defiantly try to change the season. We battle and shout, we cry and get angry, we get mad at God and turn inward, all because we don't want to admit that we're not in complete control.

In Ecclesiastes, Solomon comes to realize this lack of control and urges us to think differently about the nature of time and the seasons of life. Instead of seeing time as progressive, he understands it to be cyclical. The seasons of life come and go, then come back around again. There is plenty of time for life's activities, but each activity and task must wait for its proper season.

In Solomon's view, we can make plans but shouldn't become wed to them. We may envision progress, but we don't control the seasons of life; only God does. We can resist this fundamental truth. We can protest it. Or we can learn to relinquish control, learning to appreciate the season in which we find ourselves.

I love to play basketball. I enjoy the sport itself, and I also enjoy the competition, exercise, and adrenaline of a good game. As a young pastor I regularly played basketball with a group of guys. That ritual was important to me, and each week I devoted several hours to it. As time went on, though, the seasons of my life changed. When I started playing basketball, my wife and I had one child, I was an associate pastor at an established church, and I had maybe one evening meeting a week. These days, I have three kids, I've started and built up a new church, and I have two or three evening meetings a week. Do you see where this is going?

The seasons of my life changed, and I had some choices to make. I no longer had enough time to do all the things I wanted to do. As much as I loved basketball, I decided that giving an evening to it every week was no longer worthwhile. Instead, I began working out early in the morning, and I stopped playing basketball. Do I miss it? Absolutely. Do I wish I could do it again? Yes. But in this season of my life, I've decided that being a good husband, father, and church leader is more important.

Like a house that's been outgrown, sometimes our lives must expand as we respond to new realities. We have to patch up areas that have been neglected, seal foundations that have been ignored. There are also times in our lives when no amount of remodeling, renovation, or addition is going to be enough, when we just have to tear everything down and start over.

What season are you in? Do you need to be planting or pruning? Or do you need to conclusively stop something in your life and allow it to die? Whether involving a habit, a job, or a relationship, a season of death can be heart-wrenching. It can feel like giving up. But it often is accompanied by a season of healing, of pouring your energy into fixing and reconciling and ultimately replanting.

We've all heard the phrase "Let go and let God." It's kind of a cheesy and cliché thing to say, but I've realized that it's also kind of true. Whatever season of life you're in, you'd be amazed at what can happen when you let go of things you can't control and learn to trust in God. It's a challenge for me; it's a challenge for all of us.

As Paul puts it, "I can endure all these things through the power of the one who gives me strength" (Philippians 4:13).

What helps Paul cultivate contentment and happiness in his life, even when in prison, is that he trusts that God is in control. He believes with all his heart that God is working for his welfare and not his harm, and is creating a future with hope.

Do you hear what Paul is saying? I can hope, I can feel joy, I can find lasting happiness and a deep inner peace—all because I know that I'm not in control; God is. Tapping into God's power is what gave Paul strength even in his dark times.

Happiness and Circumstances

When our lasting happiness is rooted in God, it's easier to deal with shifting circumstances. Expressed in a different way, our happiness is more secure when it is based on our relationship with God.

We're not in control, but there's one who is. So we don't always have to smile. Our lives don't always have to be great. We can maintain hope for the future, because there's a God who does have strength, who does have vision, who is at work even in our dark circumstances. Through it all, God loves us. God cares. God is working for our welfare and not for our harm, to give us a future with hope.

Knowing this, you and I can cultivate contentment even on bad days or months or years. We know not to base our happiness on circumstances—things that are physical, temporal, external—because when we trust circumstances, we set ourselves up for disappointment. When circumstances change, our entire basis for joy and happiness is gone.

We can't trust circumstances, but we can root our hope, our trust, our peace, our joy in a God who is in control and who never fails. God's power doesn't vacillate. It doesn't change. It's present in good times and bad.

I try to read the Psalms regularly. When I do, I find—either because my memory isn't good or because Scripture is so soaked with wisdom—that I see new things each time I read them. This week, I've been studying Psalm 136, and I'm finding that it has a lot to say about happiness and circumstances. The psalmist tells us that, in contrast to all the earthly things we place our confidence in—our money, our family, our job, our achievements, all of which are fleeting, temporal, circumstantial—what we can rely on instead is God's truth, God's love, God's promises, God's presence. The psalmist exclaims that "God's faithful love lasts forever!" and feels so strongly about it that the phrase is repeated over and over again, twenty-six times!

To be clear, when I say that we should look beyond circumstances I'm not suggesting that we settle for less-than-ideal situations. I don't mean that we should stop hoping and working to make things better, or that we should cover up our pain by pretending to be in a good mood all the time. I am not suggesting that we should sugarcoat life or that we never have permission to have a bad day (or week or year). Rather, I mean that finding contentment in God will prevent our happiness from rising and falling when things change. This kind of happiness can sustain us in the worst of times and temper us in the best of times, because it is rooted in God. In a counterintuitive way, when we root our happiness and contentment in God, it actually can allow us greater freedom to feel what we need to feel on any given day, without those feelings ultimately defining us or our joy.

When our happiness is rooted in a relationship with God, we can be fully present in the moment, embracing the moment more fully with the knowledge that God is present with us, walking beside us, watching over us, and directing us.

Whether we're having a good day or a bad day, a great year or a really tough season of life, be assured that Scripture promises joy, hope, peace, and happiness in God.

So, live in the present, change your perspective, be grateful, and let go of the need to control—four steps along the path to lasting happiness. Is there one of these steps that you especially need to focus on? Make a note of it. Or maybe write down all four and let them serve as a guide.

Let's close with the Serenity Prayer, which in so many ways is about letting go of our need to control and trusting in a power greater than ourselves.

God, grant me the serenity to accept the things I cannot change,
The courage to change the things I can,
And the wisdom to know the difference. Amen.

4

A WAY OF BEING

4

A WAY OF BEING

I majored in mathematics in college, specifically theoretical or "pure" math. Essentially, that means everything I worked on was relatively abstract. Often my homework consisted of a few complicated problems to solve. The problems might take twenty minutes or two weeks; it all depended. They often required me to come up with a key insight or to see something that wasn't immediately obvious. Once I had that epiphany, the problem could be solved fairly quickly; but without the epiphany, all the hours in the world weren't going to help. Occasionally I would get a math problem that eluded me. I could not for the life of me figure out the solution. I would sit in the library struggling with a problem for hours, to no avail. Then suddenly, while taking a shower or going for a run, the insight would hit me. In a matter of minutes I would solve the problem.

The frustrating thing was that there was no way to predict the "aha" moment, and all the work in the world wouldn't manufacture the solution. As it turned out, the answer often would come to me precisely when I backed off, turned away, and focused on something else.

I've since discovered that much of life works this way. The more we focus on the solution to a problem, seek it out, stress over it, and chase after it, the more it eludes us. But sometimes when we back off and turn our attention elsewhere, it just appears.

This is often true of happiness. As we've seen, a lot of what we think will make us happy, doesn't. The more we focus on our own happiness, the more it can frustrate us. But it is precisely when we back off, when we focus on something (or someone) else, that happiness happens.

A turning point occurs in chapter 9 of Luke's Gospel. Up until that point, Jesus had spent most of his time teaching, healing people, exorcising demons, performing miracles, and gaining followers as he traveled through towns and villages. His fame was spreading rapidly, and people wanted to be a part of what Jesus was doing. But then something changed. The first clue to the change is at the beginning of chapter 9:

> *Jesus called the Twelve together and he gave*
> *them power and authority over all demons*
> *and to heal sicknesses. He sent them out to*
> *proclaim God's kingdom and to heal the sick.*
>
> *(Luke 9:1-2)*

In essence, Jesus was saying, "OK, everything that you have watched me do? Now it's your turn!" The Scriptures don't record the disciples' immediate reaction, but I have to imagine they gaped at one another. Wasn't Jesus getting this wrong? After all, he was the Messiah, and they were just followers. He was the one who did cool things, and they were the ones who got to witness the cool things. But now he was asking them to teach, heal, and cast out demons? How was that supposed to work?

In his words to the disciples, Jesus revealed that the plan all along had been for *them* to share good news in the lives of others. This surprising theme plays out in the remainder of chapter 9 and changes the rest of the story. From this point on, the work of the disciples begins to emerge. Of course, that work is most vividly on display in the sequel to the Gospel of Luke, the Book of Acts. But Luke 9 is where it starts.

Jesus Didn't Get the Memo

So, what does all this have to do with happiness? It's that, embedded in this turning-point chapter, Jesus flipped around a commonsense way in which most people view satisfaction and happiness. He challenged his disciples—and us—to be bearers of his ministry, not just receivers of it, and along the way he dropped a counterintuitive truth about life.

> *Jesus said to everyone, "All who want to come after me must say no to themselves, take up their cross daily, and follow me. All who want*

> *to save their lives will lose them. But all who*
> *lose their lives because of me will save them."*
>
> *(Luke 9:23-24)*

Wait, what? Say no to ourselves? Take up a cross? Lose our lives to save them? It sounds as strange to us as it did to the disciples. Jesus was talking about the meaning of life and God's part in it. How do we live the life that God desires for us and find lasting happiness?

Remember where we started. Happiness isn't primarily a feeling. It isn't just a temporary state of cheerfulness. In Scripture, happiness is something much deeper. It is a condition, a state of living, a way of being in the world that God desires for us. Happiness is finding wholeness, peace, and contentment. Happiness is the life that is truly life. In the Gospel of John, Jesus says his purpose on earth is to give people abundant life, the kind of life we were intended for.

> *"The thief enters only to steal, kill, and destroy.*
> *I came so that they could have life—indeed, so*
> *that they could live life to the fullest."*
>
> *(John 10:10)*

If you browse the Web for advice on finding happiness, the results will be all over the map. But many of them, in one form or another, say that to find happiness you need to focus on yourself. One website offered the following suggestions:

- Write your achievements.
- Decide to make yourself a priority.

Happiness is finding
wholeness, peace,
and contentment.
Happiness is the life
that is truly life.

- Fill your day with tiny things you love.
- Create visuals of your awesomeness.[3]

In case you're wondering, I did try creating a visual of my own awesomeness, without much success. We might laugh at that suggestion and several of the others, but in fact it's fairly common wisdom in our culture. If you want to be happy, focus on yourself and the things that make you feel good.

Now look at how radically different Jesus' advice is. Do you want happiness? Don't focus more on yourself; focus on others. Don't say yes to yourself more often; say no. Don't double down on yourself; give yourself away in service to Jesus and others.

Apparently Jesus didn't get the memo, the one that said the way to happiness in this world is to put yourself first, make yourself a priority, and visualize your own awesomeness. Jesus offers his followers a completely different path, and this path isn't about you. It's about God and the role you can play in God's work.

It's Counterintuitive

Before we discuss further what Jesus wants of us, let's consider just how strange his advice is. Find your life by losing it? That goes against the accepted worldly wisdom about happiness. It goes against our gut instincts. It goes against intuition. Usually when we are feeling down, frustrated, and stressed, our inclination is to circle the wagons, think less about others, and focus more on ourselves.

But Jesus says that happiness, like a math problem that will be solved precisely when we are not working on it, is found when we don't make it the primary focus of our lives.

Surprisingly, Jesus isn't the only one giving us this counterintuitive advice. His wisdom, it turns out, dovetails with what many experts—from therapists to sociologists to neurosurgeons to financial advisors—are finding out about human beings: though we are tempted to adopt an inward focus, happiness comes when we focus on people and things outside ourselves. You might say that one key to happiness is learning to live an inside-out life, guided by the principal that Jesus taught more than two thousand years ago: you will find your life by losing it.

In 2013, *The Wall Street Journal* published an essay that caught my eye. Titled "Hard-Wired for Giving," the article begins with this:

> The Darwinian principle of "survival of the fittest" echoes what many people believe about life: To get ahead, you need to look out for No. 1....But the latest science shows that, in fact, we are also hardwired to be generous.[4]

The article goes on to describe some of the latest scientific research related to giving money away instead of keeping it for ourselves. Scientists have found that when people are generous, giving money to causes they care about or to people in need, the brain produces the feel-good chemicals oxytocin and dopamine—some of the same chemicals turned out during other pleasurable activities such as sex. No such chemicals are produced by focusing on the self. Not only that, the scientists have also found that a cycle is established: when we practice generosity, our brain produces the chemicals, we feel great and want to be more generous, leading to more of the good chemicals and more happiness. As one scientist put it, we become addicted to giving. As tempted as we may be to hoard what we have, these scientific studies seem to indicate that we are indeed hardwired to give.

Similar results have been found by sociologists who studied lottery winners. The researchers wanted to find out if winning a fortune elevated one's level of happiness. They discovered that receiving the money produced a small increase in happiness, but the feeling was temporary. After a short period of time, winners reported happiness levels returned to the levels reported by normal folks without millions of dollars.[5] Contrary to what most of us think, a financial windfall doesn't make us happy.

Several years ago, the *U.S. News & World Report* featured a story about a new body of research on the topic of "positive activity interventions."

> Doing something nice for someone else often leaves people feeling good about themselves and positive about their place in the world.
>
> But does that mean practicing random acts of kindness has scientifically proven therapeutic value in treating mood disorders like depression?

Yes, according to a growing body of research that has found that "positive activity interventions"—like helping someone with groceries, writing a thank you note or even counting your blessings—can serve as an effective, low-cost treatment for depression.

"They seem really trivial. They seem like, what's the big deal, you feel good for 10 minutes," said Sonja Lyubomirsky, a psychology professor at the University of California, Riverside, who co-authored a recent paper on the topic. "But for a depressed person, they aren't trivial at all. Depressed individuals need to increase positive emotions in their life, even a minute here and there."[6]

The article describes the benefits people experience when they begin to focus their attention on others. This isn't to suggest that depression doesn't sometimes require medicine, therapy, and other kinds of interventions. But it does show a simple relationship between focusing on others and positive emotion in our own lives. Serving and helping others contributes to finding our own joy in life.

As Dr. Michelle Riba, former president of the American Psychiatric Association, has written, "In general, people who help others stop focusing on their own pains and problems and worries and feel good about themselves."[7]

I could give more examples, but I think you can see the parallels. Jesus isn't the only one teaching these counterintuitive truths. What we are finding out—whether from science, psychology, or anecdotal experience—is that focusing on ourselves may seem like the best path to happiness, but in fact the key to happiness is found in something (or someone) outside ourselves.

So, where should our focus be? Let's go back to what Jesus said:

> *"All who want to come after me must say no*
> *to themselves, take up their cross daily, and*
> *follow me. All who want to save their lives will*
> *lose them. But all who lose their lives because*
> *of me will save them."*
>
> *(Luke 9:23-24)*

I don't think Jesus meant that we aren't important, that our health and well-being don't matter, that we should neglect ourselves. I do think Jesus meant that real life, joyful life, is about focusing on God and the people God cares about. The principle is simple, but it's so easy to forget.

A Role in God's Story

I have a friend who recently bought a house that's more than one hundred years old. He and his wife had a vision of restoring the house and bringing it back to its former glory. They bought the house and soon began gutting it. As they got further into the project, they uncovered more and more problems. The project list grew, and the time line lengthened. Many months (and many thousands of dollars) later, they were growing weary of the project. Every day they were focused on the house—what finishes to put in, what flooring to install,

Sometimes the best thing
we can do is step outside
ourselves and remember
that there is more to the
world, and to life, than our
own stuff.... There's a
God who is up to
something more important
than making sure our
lives work out just the way
we want them to.

what tasks still needed to be done. In fact, the house project became the sole focal point of their lives.

My friend told me that finally, at a low point in the project, he was at the store one day to purchase yet one more item for the house. As he stood in line at the counter, he watched the guy in front of him checking out, and suddenly my friend just burst out and told him, "Your stuff is on me." He picked up the tab for this complete stranger's items!

As he told me the story months later (inside his home that was finished and beautiful), my friend confessed, "For months I had been so consumed by my project that I just wanted to stop spending on myself and help someone else. Buying that guy's stuff helped me regain perspective—that there was more to life than choosing the paint colors for our walls."

That's a simple example, but it illustrates the point. It's so easy to become obsessed by our jobs, stressed over our finances, consumed with our own relationship drama, or anxious about our own future. Sometimes the best thing we can do is step outside ourselves and remember that there is more to the world, and to life, than our own stuff. There are people struggling with problems far bigger than ours. There are needs much greater. There's a God who is up to something more important than making sure our lives work out just the way we want them to.

When we poke our heads up and look around, we discover that we have a role to play in God's story. Friends need our help. People are going through what we've experienced. We have gifts that can benefit others. By becoming so enmeshed in our own internal dramas, we can lose sight of why all this stuff matters. We've forgotten our greater purpose and calling.

As we refocus our eyes beyond ourselves, we see more clearly who God created us to be, we remember what gets us excited, and we discover what we have to offer. In short, we begin to be happy.

More Than a Martyr

When we study Jesus' teachings, we see that he was talking about more than simply helping others. He said that when we say no to ourselves and *follow him*, we find our life. When we lose our life *because of him*, we find it.

This isn't about becoming martyrs or neglecting ourselves or just doing what others want us to do. This isn't about serving people so they will like us. It's about focusing on Jesus and the people Jesus cares about. It's about listening for what God is up to in our lives, our neighborhood, our city, our world. It's about looking beyond what we think we need, what we think we want, and what we think our lives ought to be. It's about seeing what God wants, what God needs, what God wants our lives to be. When we readjust our thinking in this way, several things begin to happen.

1. We gain a new perspective.

The prophet Isaiah records these words:

> *My plans aren't your plans,*
> *nor are your ways my ways, says the LORD.*
> *Just as the heavens are higher than the earth,*
> *so are my ways higher than your ways,*
> *and my plans than your plans.*
> *(Isaiah 55:8-9)*

115

God sees things we cannot see. When we rely on our own plans and become consumed with the execution of those plans, we miss the larger picture of what might be possible. And when we miss the larger picture, we overlook some of the most exciting things that God has in store for us. I'll illustrate this truth with a story from my own life.

When I majored in math at Washington University, I was immersed in a competitive atmosphere, hyper-focused on what I wanted to do with my life, and anxious about a track that would lead me to something great. There was just one problem: I had no idea what I wanted to do. The closer I got to graduation, the more concerned I became. I saw friends interview for graduate school, accept job offers, and move to exciting new places. Soon it was the spring of my senior year, and my anxiety began to overwhelm me. Desperate, I decided to pray about it, so I caught a bus and headed to the Cathedral Basilica in downtown St. Louis.

I spent a long time sitting in that huge Romanesque cathedral, asking God to guide me. As I rode the bus back to my apartment, I had a strong sense that perhaps there was more I needed to explore with my faith. God didn't miraculously give me an answer to my prayer, but I did sense a nudge to stop focusing on what I wanted to be and instead commit some time to exploring what God might want me to be. That afternoon, I sent in last-minute applications to some seminaries. A few weeks later, my dad took me on a trip to visit a few of them. I decided to take a chance and attend one of them the next fall.

It took me years before God really answered that prayer, but it started when I asked a different kind of question. When

I stopped focusing on my own plans and listened for God's, it began an adventure that I never would have had on my own. As a math major, I never dreamed that I would make my living reading, writing, and talking! The last thing I could have foreseen was that God would use me to start a new church, welcome people, and cultivate leaders. By myself I would have seen none of it.

I have no idea how my life would have turned out if I hadn't made that trip to the Cathedral Basilica. But I am convinced of this: if I hadn't asked God for guidance and been open to God's intentions for me, I would have missed out on the adventure of a lifetime.

My passion is to help people gain a different perspective on their lives by connecting with God and beginning to follow Christ. I am passionate because, through Jesus, I have been given a new perspective, and it has led me to a life I wouldn't have found on my own.

2. We are used and useful.

One of the most common complaints I get from people is that they're struggling to find a purpose. They often phrase it this way: "I want to be part of something bigger than myself." Those words express an innate desire to become involved with what God is doing in the world.

When we follow Jesus, we are ushered into God's kingdom work and into a purpose that is meaningful and joy-filled. Here's how the author of Proverbs puts it: "Many plans are in a person's mind, but the Lord's purpose will succeed" (19:21).

A man in my congregation spent decades addicted to alcohol and drugs. As a functioning alcoholic, he worked, had a family, and was surrounded by friends. But he later told me that during those years he was selfish and lived out of a sense of fear—fear of failure, of being rejected, of opening himself up, of facing his emotions and feelings.

When he decided to get sober, he turned to God. As he began listening to God, the scales that had covered his eyes and heart began to fall away. God pushed him to be vulnerable, to risk himself, and most of all to say yes when opportunities arose to serve. Soon he was sharing his own story of addiction with others, agreeing to meet with anyone and everyone who was going through a similar struggle. As God used his brokenness in a redemptive way, he began feeling a sense of joy. He realized that even the darkest chapters of his life—*especially* the darkest chapters of his life—could be used by God to affect the lives of other people. He claimed a sense of his usefulness in God's kingdom, and every day he tried to let God use him more fully. As he did, he felt a greater sense of peace and joy.

3. We are directed to the things that matter most.

In his Sermon on the Mount, Jesus spoke of our tendency to become consumed with the basic necessities of life. Of course, we need food to eat and clothes to wear. But Jesus said this: "Instead, desire first and foremost God's kingdom and God's righteousness, and all these things will be given to you as well" (Matthew 6:33).

Jesus was speaking about the things in life that matter most. So many of us focus on necessary things and neglect *great* things. We need clothes, but the kind of clothes we wear isn't important. We need transportation, but the make and model of car is trivial. We need a place to live, but the lot size, square footage, and color of the granite counters don't make any difference. And yet we expend huge amounts of our time, energy, and money on such things.

When we follow Jesus, we set off down a different path. We learn about serving others and find joy when God uses us. We are invited into the practice of generosity and find that we're rewarded in countless ways. We're challenged to focus on relationships with God and others, and we begin to experience things that are more powerful than material possessions.

When we follow Jesus—when we focus on his life and listen to his words—we can experience peace and joy.

A Gift

So, what is happiness? It is an abiding sense of peace that we can experience and dwell in no matter what our circumstances. Though we may search for happiness in all sorts of places—material possessions, money, achievements, legacies, adventure—it is most robustly found in relationships. Happiness depends upon the state of three relationships: with God, with ourselves, and with others. We all know that relationships get messy. Beneath the unhappiness that most of us experience is a boatload of broken relationships. If we are to find and hold on to happiness, we have to address those relationships.

But we don't do that alone. The mission of Jesus and the reason God sent him into the world was to heal our relationships, bring us reconciliation, and give us peace. Jesus' desire is that we "have life, and have it abundantly" (John 10:10 NRSV). On the cross, Jesus reconciled us to God and healed our broken connections with the Creator. With his Spirit, Jesus gives us a renewed heart and mind to see our relationships with others differently. He offers us the beautifully painful practice of forgiveness as a way to move beyond sin in our personal relationships. He restores us to our true selves and allows us, finally, to be at peace with who we are. Jesus is not about rules and regulations. He didn't come to make our lives less fun or to keep us from doing what we want to do. Jesus came to heal and lead us toward true happiness.

When we discover these truths, we can find contentment and begin to live differently. We hear Jesus' call to give our lives away, not to maintain our own joy but to offer it to those around us, in Christ's name. Following Jesus in this way can unlock our purpose, introduce us to our calling, and help us use even our darkest moments to enrich the lives of those around us. As we serve others, Jesus continues the work of healing us and leading us into peace and joy.

And so we end where we began, with the idea that peace and joy—what I call lasting happiness—can't be found by focusing on ourselves. It's not in the stuff we accumulate, the titles we gain, or the accolades we receive. It's not a feeling that comes and goes with each day's circumstances.

Happiness is a gift. It's given to us when we trust and follow Christ. If we seek after him and commit our being to him, he leads us to people, practices, and purposes far beyond anything we could ask for or imagine. And in the process, we are saved.

Eternal God, forgive us for the times we live only for ourselves. Help us learn to give our lives away in meaningful and important ways. Guide us in that effort, so that we may find ourselves and our happiness in service to you. We pray this in the name of the one who gave his life for us, Jesus Christ our Lord. Amen.

NOTES

1. Robert Waldinger. "What makes a good life? Lessons from the longest study on happiness." Lecture, TEDxBeaconStreet, November 2015. Accessed January 2, 2017. http://www.ted.com/talks/robert_waldinger_what_makes_a_good_life_lessons_from_the_longest_study_on_happiness/transcript?language=en

2. Ibid

3. Chris Freytag, "Six Ways to Create Your Own Happiness," http://www.mindbodygreen.com/0-12605/6-ways-to-create-your-own-happiness.html, accessed January 2, 2017.

4. Elizabeth Svoboda, "Hard-Wired for Giving," *The Wall Street Journal*, http://www.wsj.com/articles/SB10001424127887324009304579041231971683854, accessed January 2, 2017.

5. Bourree Lam, "What Becomes of Lottery Winners?" *The Atlantic*, published January 12, 2016. http://www.theatlantic.com/business/archive/2016/01/lottery-winners-research/423543/, accessed January 2, 2017.

6. Dennis Thompson, "With Depression, Helping Others May in Turn Help You," *U.S. News & World Report*, http://health .usnews.com/health-news/family-health/brain-and-behavior /articles/2012/01/02/with-depression-helping-others-may-in -turn-help-you, accessed January 2, 2017.
7. Ibid.

ACKNOWLEDGMENTS

I never considered myself an author or set out to write a book. In fact, I was surprised to be called into ministry. As a math guy, I wouldn't have guessed that God would call me to use two skills that I thought were my weaknesses: writing and speaking. Yet that is what I do. But I certainly wouldn't be here without the help of so many.

I have to start with my parents and the small church in Washington, Missouri, where I was raised. My parents taught me what it means to be faithful and committed, and the people of Washington First United Methodist Church planted my faith, nurtured its growth, and in due time affirmed a call to ministry in my life.

I am grateful to those who believed in this book and encouraged me to write, beginning with the people at my church, The Gathering, in St. Louis. In my sermons and my writing, they always let me know what resonates and what doesn't, and they are the most encouraging congregation a pastor could serve. I am extraordinarily blessed to serve with a board at The Gathering that sees part of its mission as affecting the greater church; because of its wise vision, the board grants me the time and space for projects with a broader reach. I am grateful to my staff members at The Gathering. They give me the freedom and opportunity to write, and they make me look much better than I actually am. I am grateful to my assistant, Amy Sanders, who keeps me moving forward and without whom the book deadlines would have been blown.

I am grateful to Susan Salley and Ron Kidd at Abingdon Press, who believed in this project, urged me to write, guided me along the way, and worked the manuscript through to completion. The book simply wouldn't have happened without them.

Finally, I am grateful to my three kids, Caleb, Carly, and George, and most of all to my wife, Jessica. They sacrifice much in service to my calling. They give up time with me so that I can spend it writing and working on books such as this one. They get far too little acknowledgment as a key part of my ministry. It really is a family ministry, and they contribute to it in ways that are crucial but largely unseen.

For anything in this book that helps you, the credit goes to God and to the great people who surround me. The errors and shortcomings are mine alone.